100 GREATEST GOLFERS

100 GREATEST GOLFERS

IAN MORRISON

Bison Books

Published by
Bison Books Ltd
176 Old Brompton Road
London SW5 0BA
England

ISBN 0-86124-427-3

Printed in Hong Kong

Pages 2-3: The 1987 US Open at the
Olympic Club, San Francisco.

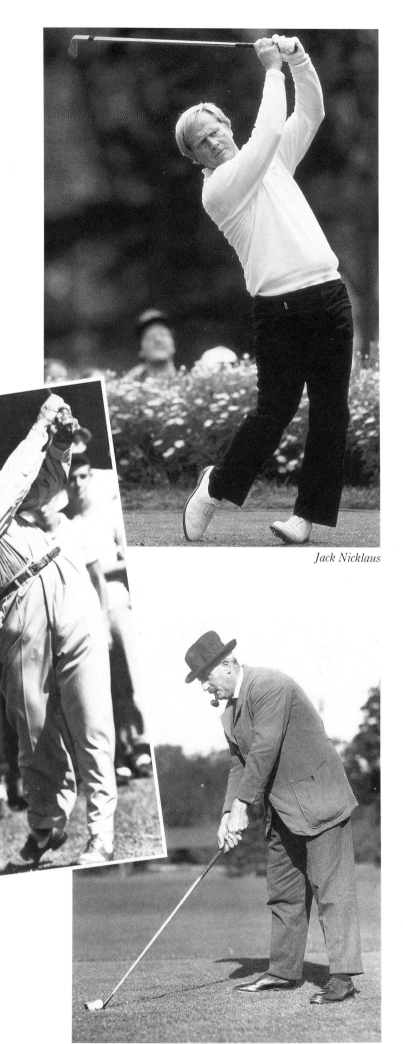

Jack Nicklaus

Sam Snead

Severiano Ballesteros

Ted Ray

Contents

J H Taylor

Gary Player

Francis Ouimet

Byron Nelson

Isao Aoki

Introduction

Writing a book about the world's 100 greatest golfers does not, at first, seem a particularly difficult task, because over the last 120 years many great names have provided excellent material for journalists and authors.

It's easy to begin reeling off names – men like Jack Nicklaus, Arnold Palmer, Bobby Jones and Walter Hagen come to mind immediately. But where do you stop? Once you have listed the really big names you are left with plenty of golfers on the fringes of the top 100. Deciding which of these should be included is where the difficulty begins.

Playing records seem an obvious criterion for assessing a golfer's ability. But if you look at a golfer like Tom Kite, who has never won a major championship in his career yet remains one of the biggest money winners of all time, you need to ask whether records alone are a suitable criterion. Because once you ask whether Kite should go in the answer is an unqualified Yes.

So it's virtually impossible to produce a definitive list of the all-time 100 greatest golfers. Any choice will inevitably cause controversy. Ian Woosnam and Paul Azinger, for example, are included. Why, you might ask? You have only to look at their outstanding performances in 1987 alone to see the reason. And when you consider the level of competition these days, compared to the level that Harry Vardon, Ted Ray and James Braid faced at the turn of the century, you realize that the modern-day golfer is inevitably measured by a different type of 'greatness.'

When it came down to the final choice I went for a mixture of golfers who had enjoyed long careers or successful careers, or who had made an impact of some sort during their spell in the game.

I don't expect you to agree with my choice, but I do expect you to agree with me that making such a choice was not easy.

Ian Morrison

Peter Alliss

With his formidable knowledge of the game, Peter Alliss has become one of Britain's foremost golfing experts. A gifted player, his most notable successes occurred during the late 1950s.

Alliss was born in Germany, where his father Percy was serving as a professional. He soon showed outstanding ability, gaining junior international honors at 15. Before he was 16 he had turned professional.

In 1953 Alliss followed in his father's footsteps when he joined the British Ryder Cup team to play the first of eight matches between 1953 and 1969. His debut, was, however, to prove disastrous. In his crucial singles with Jim Turnesa he took four putts from the edge of the green at Wentworth's 18th hole. Turnesa won the hole and their battle; the United States went on to win the Cup by just one match.

It was several years before Alliss recovered from this setback, but his performance improved considerably after he joined the Parkstone (Dorset) Golf Club in 1955. There he developed a classic swing, although his game often suffered because of his erratic and inconsistent putting. In 1956, ten years after turning professional, he won his first big title, the Spanish Open. Then in 1958 he enjoyed his most successful season when he carried off the Open titles of Portugal, Italy and, for the second time, Spain. But apart from winning the British PGA title in 1962 and 1965, very few titles were to come Alliss's way again.

In 1962 he was elected captain of the PGA and a year later the first of his many golf books, *Alliss Through the Looking Glass*, was published. He moved to Moor Allerton, Yorkshire in 1970 and has since become one of the best tutors and most respected television commentators in the world. Alliss was honored with the captaincy of the PGA for a second time in 1987.

BELOW: *Peter Alliss in his customary role behind the microphone. One of the game's great tutors, his love and knowledge of the game have earned him considerable respect in the golfing world.*

Willie Anderson

Isao Aoki

With over 50 wins in his home country Isao Aoki is the most successful golfer in Japan today. He holds the further distinction of being the first Japanese golfer to win on the US Tour.

Born in Abiko in 1942, Aoki realized at an early stage of his career the importance of being both a good short-game player and a good putter. He used to spend hours developing these aspects of his game at the Abiko Golf Club where he worked as a caddie.

In 1964 when he was 21 he turned professional but had to wait seven years before his first success, the Kanto PGA title. After several highly successful years

LEFT: *Scottish-born Willie Anderson, who became in 1905 the only person to win the US Open three years in succession. He also won the title in 1901.*

RIGHT: *Isao Aoki kisses the ball after scoring a hole-in-one at the 1979 Suntory World Match-Play Championship at Wentworth.*
BELOW: *Aoki in pensive mood lining up a putt.*

Willie Anderson shares with Bobby Jones, Ben Hogan and Jack Nicklaus the rare distinction of having won the US Open four times. However, Willie Anderson was the only man to win the coveted title three years in succession.

Born in Scotland in 1878, Willie first learned to play golf when he moved with his family to the United States in the mid-1890s. His career got off to an impressive start when, in his first Open, he finished runner-up to Joe Lloyd at Chicago in 1897. Four years later Willie became champion after beating Alex Smith in a play-off at Myopia Hunt.

His remarkable hat-trick of wins began at Baltusrol in 1903 when, again, he won after a play-off, beating David Brown by two strokes. Next in 1904 he won by five shots from Gilbert Nicholls at Glen View, Illinois, establishing a new championship record with a final round 72. He completed the hat-trick a year later with a two-shot win over Alex Smith at Myopia Hunt. In all four wins, Anderson never recorded a four-round total under 300, although had he used modern equipment the figure would have been nearer 280.

Anderson continued playing championship golf right up to his death in 1910, winning the Western Open only a year before he died. Had it not been for his untimely departure, he might well have held the record for US Open wins outright.

in his home country, when he became the biggest money winner of all time in Japan, Aoki decided to spend time on the US and European circuits.

In Europe he won the 1978 World Match-Play title at Wentworth, beating New Zealand's Simon Owen 3 and 2 in the final. The following year he narrowly failed to retain his title when American Bill Rogers beat him by one hole. He did have some consolation though – his hole-in-one against David Graham won him a furnished flat at Gleneagles valued at £55,000. His other European success was the 1983 European Open at Sunningdale. There is some irony in the fact that the Open was for the first time being sponsored by a Japanese electronics company.

But it was in the United States in 1983 that Aoki was to experience what he later described as 'the greatest thrill of my career.' Three years before, in 1980, he had come close to taking the US Open at Baltusrol. Paired with Jack Nicklaus for all four rounds, he had finished just two shots behind the 'Golden Bear' after three opening rounds of 68 each. Then in 1983 in the Hawaiian Open he holed out from the rough from 124 yards for an eagle at the 18th. He had become the first golfer from Japan to win on the US Tour.

Tommy Armour

Tommy Armour had to overcome a tremendous physical handicap to become one of the most outstanding golfers in the period between the two world wars. He holds the further unique distinction of having played in the forerunners of both the Walker Cup and Ryder Cup – but for different countries.

Born in Edinburgh in 1896, he lost the sight of one eye during the First World War while serving with the Tank Corps. After adjusting to his physical handicap he resumed his amateur golfing career. Armour was selected to play in the British team against the United States at Hoylake in 1921 in the forerunner to the Walker Cup. He decided to remain in the States and three years later he turned professional.

Within seven years he had won all three of the world's major tournaments (the Masters had not yet been inaugurated at the time). However, before he won his first major, Armour had been selected for the US team in the first unofficial Ryder Cup match against Great Britain at Wentworth in 1926. A year later he won the US Open by beating Harry Cooper by three shots in a play-off at Oakmont.

ABOVE: *Tommy Armour during the 1930 US PGA Championship at Fresh Meadow, New York. Armour went on to win the final, beating Gene Sarazen.*

His next major win was in the 1930 US PGA when he beat Gene Sarazen in a classic final, sinking a 14-foot putt at the 36th hole to clinch the title. The following year saw him win his one and only British Open title. His victory over the Argentinian Jose Jurado was in the first championship at Carnoustie, just 50 miles from where he was born. Armour's triumph was witnessed by the then Prince of Wales.

Tommy Armour was an outstanding golfer – his iron play and putting style were superb and his driving impeccable. He was also recognized as one of the game's great teachers. Armour wrote several authoritative books on the game, including *How to Play Your Best Golf All the Time*, which later became classics among golf students.

Although he died in 1968, his grandson, Tommy Armour III, has continued to keep the family name alive by playing regularly on the European Tour.

Paul Azinger

Paul Azinger's career has made rapid strides since 1985. Had it not been for a stroke of bad luck he might well have shared with Tony Lema the honor of winning the British Open on his first attempt.

Azinger was born in 1960 and turned professional at 21. Although he graduated from the US Tour qualifying school in 1983, he returned at the end of 1984 to improve his game. His endeavors were rewarded when he climbed from 144th to 93rd on the money list, and in 1986 he made a massive jump to 29th, thanks to five top three finishes. His best result was finishing second behind Corey Pavin, in the Hawaiian Open.

But Paul Azinger's career really took off in 1987 when he won the Phoenix Open, to give him his first Tour win. He followed that with wins in the Las Vegas Invitational and Greater Hartford Open. In 1987, too, Azinger came frustratingly close to taking the British Open. At the halfway stage on the final day he was on course to win his first major title. Then he started making mistakes. At the 17th he drove into a bunker, which resulted in a bogey six, and when he went into the 18th his three-shot lead over Britain's Nick Faldo had disappeared. Azinger failed to make the par needed to force a play-off and for the first time in three days he was no longer the leader, leaving Faldo to collect the coveted trophy. He ended the season triumphantly, however, with three US Tour wins and in second position (to Curtis Strange) on the money list.

LEFT and ABOVE: *Paul Azinger burst onto the US scene in 1987, winning three tournaments and finishing second on the money list. He is seen (left) in the Masters at Augusta and (above) at Muirfield suffering an agonizing moment when he missed a putt for second place in the British Open.*

John Ball

Born in 1861, John Ball was the first of the great amateur players to challenge the dominance of the professionals at the end of the last century.

When he was only eight years old the course at Hoylake was opened. Because his father was the owner of the Royal Hotel which served as the first clubhouse for the Royal Liverpool Golf Club, Ball soon took an interest in the game. In 1878, when he was only 16 years old, he competed in the British Open at Prestwick, finishing a commendable fourth, only eight strokes behind the winner and ahead of many famous Scottish professionals at the time.

In 1888 he won the first of his British amateur titles when he beat Johnny Laidlay 5 and 4. Between then and 1912 he won a record eight titles, including three at Hoylake. Remarkably, during that period he spent three years fighting in the Boer War with the Cheshire Yeomanry during which time he played no golf at all.

In 1890 he completed a notable double when he won

both the Amateur Championship and the Open. In winning the Open at Prestwick he not only became the first amateur winner of the coveted British Open but also the first Englishman to win the Open, thus ending a 29-year monopoly by Scottish golfers.

Ball dominated amateur golf for nearly a quarter of a century. His style and swing approached perfection, and he possessed a rare ability to play long irons into the pin. In 1921 he played in his last Amateur Championship, appropriately at his home course. Six years later, at St Andrews, he played in the British Open at the age of 65. The championship was won by the great amateur of the day, Bobby Jones who led by six strokes. Ball retired to a farm at Holywell, North Wales, where he died in December 1940.

Severiano Ballesteros

If one had to single out one golfer as the dominant player of the 1980s most people would agree on Severiano Ballesteros. Not only has he won repeatedly on the European Tour but he has made a significant impact on the tough United States Tour too. Furthermore, every year bookmakers have no hesitation in making Seve one of the favorites for the majors.

The son of a farmer, Seve was born at Pedrena, Northern Spain, in 1957. The family home was situated next to the local golf course and Seve and his three brothers, Manuel, Baldomero and Vicente, all played golf. The sport had been in the blood of the family for a long time – Uncle Ramon had been a top class professional and had finished sixth behind Jack Nicklaus in the 1965 US Masters. Seve used to caddy for his brother Manuel, who turned professional in 1969. Seve himself turned professional when he was 16, and became his country's youngest ever professional golfer.

He joined the European Tour in 1974; by the end of the 1976 season he was the top money winner after winning his first two tournaments, the Dutch Open and the Lancôme Trophy. More importantly, he gained worldwide attention that year following his performance in the British Open at Birkdale when he finished level second with Jack Nicklaus, six shots behind Johnny Miller. He was being hailed as the world's most exciting player since Arnold Palmer.

For the next two seasons Seve remained top of the money list as he became one of the world's most consistent and feared golfers. His power with the driver was awesome, even if that power did occasionally lead to some erratic shots. Ballesteros became a master of recovery shots – on one occasion he actually played from the tarmac of a car park!

To prove his true ability Seve took on the cream of American golfers in 1978 and came from 10 shots behind at the halfway stage to win the Greater Greensboro Open, the first of five wins on the US Tour. He became a regular member of the US Tour in 1984, but because he did not compete in the requisite 15 tournaments the following year, his 'ticket' was taken away.

After his performance at Birkdale in 1976, the world's leading golf experts were predicting it would only be a matter of time before Seve won his first major. They were right. In 1979 he beat Jack Nicklaus and Ben Crenshaw by three shots to win his first British Open, at Lytham, and the following year at Augusta he collected his first coveted green jacket as winner of the US Masters when he won by four shots from Jack Newton and Gibby Gilbert.

A second Masters title followed in 1983, and in 1984 he beat off a challenge from his great rival Bernhard Langer, and Tom Watson, to win his second British Open, this time at St Andrews. Ballesteros stood a

ABOVE: *Seve acknowledges the applause of the large gallery as he wins his first British Open, at Royal Lytham and St Annes in 1979.*

13

LEFT: *The determination shows as Severiano Ballesteros completes a classic upright swing.*

RIGHT: *'You're mine again.' Seve photographed after winning the British Open for a second time, at St Andrews in 1984.*

BELOW: *Ballesteros, the master of recovery shots, playing out of a trap during the 1985 Masters at Augusta.*

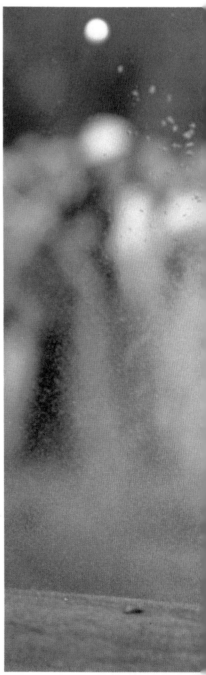

good chance of winning his third Masters in 1986. But he put his approach shot at Augusta's 15th into the lake, and a bogey there and at the next hole let Jack Nicklaus in to win his record sixth title.

During the 1986 season, however, Seve took his European career earnings past the £1 million mark, the first man to do so on the European Tour. His total of £240,000 for the year, which made him top money-winner for the fourth time since 1976, was also a record and when he tied the end-of-season Lancôme Trophy with Bernhard Langer it was the fiftieth win of his career worldwide.

Among his other distinguished successes are the World Match-Play Title four times between 1981 and 1985; the World Cup with Manuel Pinero in 1976 and with Antonio Garrido in 1977; and playing in the successful Ryder Cup team at the Belfry in 1985; and at Muirfield Village in 1987 where his fine performance helped him clinch victory for the Europeans.

Andy Bean

In 1976, just a year after turning professional, Andy Bean joined the Tour and, except for his Rookie season, he won over $100,000 every season, until a disappointing year in 1987 when his winnings dropped to $75,000. Even when he missed half the 1981 season because of a fractured thumb, he still managed to finish 35th on the list. His rise in the money-winning stakes has been very rapid, from 139th in his first season to third only two years later.

Andy was born into golf in Lafayette, Georgia, where his father was attached to a club. When Andy was 15 the family moved to Lakeland, Florida, and his father *bought* a golf course. The advantages of being able to practice freely on the course reaped their rewards when Bean won the 1977 Doral-Eastern Open. Since then he has come close to winning both the PGA Championship and the British Open. In 1980 the 6-foot 4-inch golfer finished second to Jack Nicklaus in the PGA Championship at Oak Hill, and in 1983 he came through with a final round 67 at Birkdale to tie for second place with Hale Irwin, just one shot behind Tom Watson.

Julius Boros

When he decided to abandon his career in accountancy and turn to professional golf in 1950 Julius Boros was 30 years of age. But despite his years he won the US Open two years later and, remarkably, was still winning majors in his 49th year. He was able to stay at the top for such a long time because of his superb swing.

ABOVE: *From accountancy to golf at the age of 30 – the switch certainly paid off for Julius Boros.*
LEFT: *Andy Bean after winning the 1986 Isuzu Kapalua International at Maui, Hawaii. Note how wife Debbie has already gotten her hands on the check!*

Thanks largely to his four-shot win over Porky Oliver in the US Open Julius Boros was top money winner in 1952 (a feat he repeated in 1955). It was to take 11 years before he won his second Open, when he emerged the victor from a three-way play-off involving Arnold Palmer and Jacky Cupit. At 43 years 3 months he became the oldest American winner of the title. Five years later he established another record when he became the oldest ever winner of the PGA title, beating Arnold Palmer and Bob Charles by one stroke in the 50th year of the championship.

The following year in 1969 Boros was beaten in the play-off in the Greater Greensboro Open by Gene Littler. Littler deprived him of glory once again in 1975 by winning the play-off for the Westchester Classic.

For someone who did not arrive on the professional scene until late in life, Julius Boros can look back on a fine and successful career. When he joined the Seniors Tour he won the PGA Seniors title in 1971 and 1977. And in 1977, 27 years after his first professional win, he became the 14th man in history to pass the $1 million mark when he tied 59th at Pleasant Valley.

James Braid

At the turn of the century golf was dominated by three men – Harry Vardon, John Taylor and James Braid – who collectively became known as the 'Great Triumvirate.' To this day Braid remains one of the greatest golfing figures of all time. Calm and imperturbable, he will go down in history for some outstanding records achieved within a remarkably short space of time.

Born in 1870, he left school at the age of 13 to become an apprentice joiner. He was soon invited to London to become an apprentice club-maker for the Army and Navy Stores and in 1893 turned professional. He was not a long hitter at first, but the extra length came in time and with practice.

In 1894 he competed in his first British Open but failed to find a place among the leaders. After becoming professional at Romford, Essex, in 1896 Braid competed the following year in the Open at Hoylake, finishing second to Harold Hilton. His application and determination were rewarded in 1901 when he won the British Open for the first time, beating Vardon at Muirfield by three shots. This win proved the first of many.

RIGHT: *One of golf's greats, James Braid. Along with J H Taylor and Harry Vardon, Braid dominated golf in the early part of the century.*
BELOW: *James Braid displaying his mastery of the bunker shot.*

In the ten years that followed, Braid's achievements were to multiply. He became the first man to win five Opens, his second victory coming at St Andrews in 1905 when he beat Taylor by five shots. A year later he retained the title at Muirfield, again beating Taylor, by four shots. When he won his fourth championship in 1908 his winning score of 291 was an Open record that remained unbeaten until 1927, and then it was the great Bobby Jones who bettered his record. In 1910 Braid won the Open for the fifth time with a comfortable margin of four shots.

After his retirement he remained much in demand as a golf course designer and was involved in the design, or re-design, of several courses, including Carnoustie, Gleneagles and Royal Blackheath. In 1950 Braid died and was elected an honorary member of the R and A.

Gay Brewer

A professional since 1956, Gay Brewer was a much respected member of the US Tour for nearly 30 years, and one of the world's most consistent golfers during the early 1960s.

Born in Ohio in 1932, Brewer won the US Junior Championship in 1949 but failed to win any major honors as an amateur. In his first year as a professional he joined the US Tour but had to wait until 1961 for his first win, the Carling Open. That year he won three tournaments, finishing seventh on the money list with earnings totaling $31,000.

Brewer could boast a distinctive looping swing, but on more than one occasion his putting was to let him down. One such occasion was the 1966 Masters. Brewer needed a four at the 72nd hole at Augusta to win his first major. Instead he took a five and a three-way play-off with Jack Nicklaus and Tommy Jacobs followed. Brewer's disappointing putting produced a 78; the title went to Nicklaus and Brewer had to content himself with third position.

A year later Brewer gained revenge when he beat his playing partner Bobby Nichols in a tense finish to win the title by one stroke. To crown a memorable 1967 he won the coveted Alcan Golfer of the Year Championship at St Andrews (a title he retained the following year) and gained the first of his two Ryder Cup selections, the second occurring in 1973.

Brewer won a total of eleven Tour events, the last being the 1972 Canadian Open. Although he had been on the US Tour for a long time, it was not until he joined the Seniors Tour in 1982 that he took his career earnings past the $1 million mark.

ABOVE: *Anguish . . . Until this missed putt Brewer was the sole leader in the 1966 US Masters.*
ABOVE LEFT: *Gay Brewer competing in the 1967 World Match-Play Championship at Wentworth, Surrey. The South African, Gary Player, won at the 39th hole.*

Jack Burke

Jack Burke captained the US Ryder Cup team on two occasions but he is one of the very few captains of the US team to have led the losing side. That was in 1957 when the British team won at Lindrick. As nonplaying captain at Muirfield in 1973 he turned the tables by leading the USA to a great six-point win. A hand injury meant Burke had to retire prematurely from tournament golf in the early 1960s, but in his brief spell at the top he played in some memorable matches.

Born in Texas in 1923, he turned professional at 17 but it was not until completion of his service in the Marines, and after several jobs as a working professional, that he joined the US Tour in 1950. Between then and 1956 he notched up an impressive record.

An outstanding putter, he gained Ryder Cup selection in 1951 and the following year won the Texas Open. He followed that up with successive wins in the Houston, Baton Rouge and St Petersburg Opens. Only one man has won more than four successive tournaments on the US Tour, and that was Byron Nelson, with an amazing record of 11. Burke also finished runner-up to Sam Snead in the 1952 Masters. Playing in dreadful conditions, Burke was the only man to return a score under 70 in the final round.

He enjoyed his best year in 1956 by winning both the Masters, again in appalling conditions, and the US PGA titles. At Augusta he made up eight shots on amateur Ken Venturi to win the title by one. In the PGA he came from behind in both the semifinal and final to win the then match-play title by beating Ted Kroll 3 and 2.

Between 1950 and 1963 he won 15 Tour events, and more than $250,000 in prize money. When he finished playing he concentrated on running the Champions Club in Texas with Jimmy Demaret.

LEFT: *Jack Burke playing an approach shot to the green. Burke had the honor of captaining the 1957 Ryder Cup team – in a rare defeat the team lost to Britain. It took nearly 30 years before the team suffered defeat again, this time at the Belfry in 1985 to a team led by Tony Jacklin.*

Billy Casper

Billy Casper's total of 51 Tour wins has only been bettered by five men – Snead, Nicklaus, Hogan, Palmer and Nelson. In a career spanning more than 30 years he was the first man to win $200,000 in one season, and between 1957 and 1971 he never figured lower than 11th on the US money list.

The father of 11 children, Casper was born in San Diego in 1931. In 1959, five years after turning professional, he won his first major. It was the US Open, and thanks to a great run of putting he won by one from Bob Rosburg. He regained the title at San Francisco's Olympic Club in 1966, but in dramatic style. On this occasion, with nine to play he pulled back a seven-shot lead by Arnold Palmer to force a play-off; the next day Casper won, four strokes ahead of Palmer.

When he won his third major in 1970 it was just before his 39th birthday. He beat fellow San Diegan Gene Littler in a play-off to win the Masters – which more than made up for the previous year's disappointment, when he went out in 40 on the final day and lost narrowly by just one stroke.

Winning three majors only tells part of the Billy Casper story. He has been a Ryder Cup player on eight occasions and a nonplaying captain as well. In 1981 he joined the US Seniors Tour and he won the coveted US Seniors title the same year.

LEFT: *Billy Casper playing in the 1987 Masters at Augusta, 17 years after he won the title for the only time.*

Bob Charles

New Zealand's Bob Charles is the world's greatest left-handed golfer and his putting style is among the best in golfing history. Not only has he played most of the world's golfing circuits but he has been a winner on most. His list of achievements also includes five wins on the US Tour between 1963 and 1974.

A simple swing and a devastating short-game have kept Bob Charles at the top of the game for more than 25 years. Both his parents were left-handed golfers and he followed in their footsteps, but with far more success. As an 18-year-old amateur he won the New Zealand Open in 1954. He turned professional in 1960 and won the following year's New Zealand PGA title, as well as the first of nine European Tour events, the Bowmaker Tournament.

His greatest moment was at Royal Lytham in 1963 when he beat Phil Rodgers in a 36-hole play-off to carry off golf's greatest prize, the British Open. With this

ABOVE: *Bob Charles, undoubtedly the world's finest left-handed golfer. He is also the best and most successful golfer to have come from New Zealand.*

victory Bob became the first, and only, left-hander to win the coveted trophy. Charles came close to winning the Open on two more occasions. At Carnoustie in 1968 he tied for second place, two shots behind Gary Player. That year he was also one shot behind Julius Boros in the US PGA, his best performance in an American major. In the 1969 Open at Lytham, Charles trailed home second behind Britain's Tony Jacklin. At the end of that year, however, he won the World Match-Play title by beating Gene Littler at the 37th, after sinking a 27-foot putt at the 36th hole.

A former bank clerk and now a successful sheep farmer in New Zealand, Charles continues to play on the US Seniors Tour which he joined in 1986.

Harry Cooper

Born in Surrey, England, Harry Cooper left Britain to settle in Illinois. As a golfer his trademark was the speed with which he moved around the golf course.

When he was only 18 he won the Texas Professional Open in 1923, and over the next 20 years he went on to win 20 tournaments in the United States. However, Harry Cooper will go down in golfing history as the 'nearly-man' – it is estimated he came second in as many tournaments as he won.

Perhaps his closest 'near miss' was in the 1927 US Open at Oakmont. Tommy Armour birdied from 10 feet at the 72nd hole and Cooper had two putts for the title . . . he took three and then lost the play-off. Then in the 1936 Masters he was leading Horton Smith by three shots when he went into the final round. Cooper fired a 76, Smith a 72, and Cooper was runner-up again, by one shot. To complete a disappointing year, he narrowly missed winning the US Open at Baltusrol, Ben Hogan's first Open. Although he had a lead of four as he went into the final round he lost to Tony Manero.

By contrast, his 1937 season was highly successful. He won nine events and finished top money-winner in the United States with $14,138. He also won the Canadian Open, regarded as the 'Fifth Major,' for the second time, adding to his triumph five years before.

BELOW: *Harry Cooper wearing a trilby.*

Henry Cotton's contribution to golf during his 30-year playing career was immense. In the 30 years since his retirement his contribution has been just as great – he has been the perfect tutor and has inspired many of today's players, some of whom rank among Europe's leading golfers.

Born in Cheshire in 1907, he turned professional in 1924 and was appointed assistant at Fulwell before taking up a similar position at Rye. He obtained his first post at the age of 19 when appointed professional at Langley Park, Beckenham. His outstanding talent was soon recognized by the Ryder Cup selection committee who picked him for the 1929 team to play the United States at Moortown. Cotton was able to beat Al Watrous 4 and 3 in his singles to help Great Britain to a 7-5 win. Altogether Cotton played in three Ryder Cup matches including as playing captain in 1947. He was also nonplaying captain in 1953.

Henry Cotton

The year after his Ryder Cup debut, he won his first major professional tournament in 1930, the Mar del Plata Open held in Argentina.

That same year Cotton won his first European Open when he took the Belgian title. This was to mark the start of his dominance of the European golfing scene in the years leading up to the war.

Cotton next took a post abroad, at Belgium's Waterloo Club, and it was while he was there that he won the first of his three British Open titles, at Sandwich in 1934, beating South African Sid Brews by five shots. His second round total of 65 remained an Open record for 43 years – it was only in 1977 that Tom Watson and Jack Nicklaus were able to set a new record at Turnberry. When he won his second Open, at Carnoustie in 1937, it was by two strokes from his Ryder Cup teammate Reg Whitcombe. Cotton was the professional at Ashridge, near Berkhamsted at the time.

ABOVE *The finest British golfer of the prewar era, Henry Cotton, tees off at the 4th at Sandwich on his way to winning his first of three Opens, in 1934.*

The war deprived Cotton of five vital years in his career but he put his talents to good use raising money for the Red Cross. He was later awarded the MBE for his efforts.

In 1948 he became the only man to win the Open both before and after the war when, at Muirfield, he won the title for the third time by beating the defending champion Fred Daly into second place by a massive five strokes. In 1956, and in his 50th year, Cotton finished joint sixth in the Open at Hoylake.

Since then, he has given much back to the sport in his role of course designer and teacher. His golf schools in Spain and Portugal have been the starting points for many of today's top European professionals.

Bruce Crampton

At the age of 21 Bruce Crampton was the Australian Open champion. In 1956 the often outspoken Australian visited Britain before accepting an invitation to play in the Masters at Augusta the following year. He paid a return visit to the USA in 1959 and decided to remain there as a regular and much respected member of the Tour for more than 15 years.

Although Crampton lacked a powerful drive he made up for this with his delicate play on the green.

His skillful play was to bring him close to winning a major on four occasions – only to be deprived each time by the top golfer of the day, Jack Nicklaus. Crampton's best attempt was in the 1963 PGA Championship. When he went into the final round he was leading Nicklaus by three. Crampton shot a 74, his worst round of the tournament, while Nicklaus shot 68 to relegate Bruce to joint third.

Crampton was runner-up to Nicklaus in three more majors. At Pebble Beach in the 1972 US Open the 'Golden Bear' won by three and in the PGA the following year Nicklaus beat Crampton by four strokes after posting three rounds under 70. Despite a championship record of 63 in the 1975 PGA Crampton had to be content with second place again.

In the late 1960s and early 1970s, Crampton was one of the top money winners on the US circuit. Had it not been for the presence of Nicklaus, Palmer and Player, greater glories would have fallen upon the Australian. As it was, he won 15 Tour events and was the Vardon Trophy winner in 1973 and 1975. In 1973 he became the fifth golfer in history and the first non-American to take his earnings past $1 million.

In 1977 he retired to spend more time with his family and develop his oil and gas business. He became eligible for the Seniors Tour in 1985 and, despite barely touching a golf club for a period of eight years, he soon returned to winning ways. His 1987 earnings alone were in excess of $250,000.

RIGHT: *Bruce Crampton, one of the many top-class golfers who have come from Australia. During the 1960s and 1970s he spent 15 years playing in the United States. In 1985 he returned to winning ways as a member of the popular Seniors Tour.*

Ben Crenshaw

When Ben Crenshaw walked up the 18th fairway during the 1987 British Open, the Muirfield crowd responded with applause that was as long as it was warm. Although he was out of contention for the title he was as popular as ever both sides of the Atlantic.

Born in Austin, Texas, in 1952, Ben Crenshaw got off to a promising start when he became NCAA champion three years in succession, in 1971, 1972 and 1973. In 1973 he turned professional and came through the qualifying school that fall.

In 1973 Crenshaw won the very first tournament he played in as a professional, the Texas Open. He finished second in his next event, the $500,000 World Open, and in 1974 he was Rookie of the Year. Three wins in the 1976 season took him to second position on the money list, just $9000 behind winner Jack Nick-

ABOVE: *Texan Ben Crenshaw is one of the game's most respected golfers, admired by fans and fellow professionals alike on both sides of the Atlantic.*

laus. He has since remained among the top 25 every year with the exception of 1982 and 1985. In 1985, after slipping to 149 in the rankings, he was diagnosed as having a thyroid disorder. Once diagnosed, he came bouncing back with a vengeance to finish in the top ten in both 1986 and 1987.

The greatest moment in the career of Ben Crenshaw came in 1984 when he won his one and only major, the Masters. After the first round at Augusta he was leading, but over the next two days he slipped back. A four-under-par 68 on the final round saw him win a very popular victory by two from Tom Watson.

Jimmy Demaret

It is not often that a golfer wins six tournaments in a single year on the US Tour. And when that person is a nightclub singer and his wins include the Masters, then it is an even more remarkable achievement.

That is exactly what Texan Jimmy Demaret did in 1940 when he emerged as the outstanding golfer of the year. In an era when there were many up-and-coming players the much respected Demaret swept all before him. His four-stroke victory in the Masters was aided by a first round 67 in which he covered the back nine in a staggering 30 shots.

Born in 1910 into a large Texan family, the son of a carpenter/painter, Demaret was taking a gamble when he turned professional. At the time the rewards from golf were nowhere near as great as they are today. His first tutor was Jack Burke Senior who employed the young golfer as his assistant in 1926. By the time he was 22 Demaret was professional at Galveston.

After his 1940 victory Demaret won a second Masters title in 1947. In 1950 he became the first man to win the coveted trophy three times when he hauled back Jim Ferrier's five-shot lead with six to play to

ABOVE: *Jimmy Demaret putting during the 1940 San Francisco Open. Did it or didn't it go in? Judging by the expressions on the fans' faces it is not easy to tell.*

eventually win by two shots. Although he didn't win any other majors he was runner-up in the 1948 US Open to Ben Hogan. And in 1957, at the age of 47, he finished third, just one stroke behind Dick Mayer and Cary Middlecoff.

Demaret's record in the Ryder Cup is the best in Ryder Cup history. Twice he teamed up with Ben Hogan in the foursomes and won both times. He played in 1947, 1949 and 1951 and won not only all three foursomes, but all three singles too.

During his successful career Jimmy Demaret won 31 Tour events. In 1947 he was the top money winner and he was also awarded the Vardon Trophy that year. Once his playing days were over, the man who was easily identified by his brightly colored clothing became joint owner of the Champions Club at Houston with his friend Jack Burke Junior. Demaret died of a heart attack in December 1983.

Roberto de Vicenzo

When Roberto de Vicenzo visited Britain for the first time in 1948 to compete in the Open at Muirfield he finished joint third behind Henry Cotton. Between then and 1969, however, he established a tremendous record in the championship, finishing in the top three no fewer than eight times. During his long career he has won more than 150 professional tournaments including 40 national championships.

Born in Buenos Aires in 1923, de Vicenzo came from a poor family and he and his brothers, all of whom were later to turn professional, used to earn extra money by caddying. When he was 15 Roberto became a pro and in 1947 he ventured to the United States.

In 1950 he was runner-up to Bobby Locke at Troon; then playing at Hoylake in 1967, at the age of 44, he became the oldest winner of the title this century. Final rounds of 67 and 70 fought off a challenge from Jack Nicklaus, as the likeable and friendly Argentinian became a very popular winner by two strokes.

A year after his Hoylake win, de Vicenzo was deprived of a possible US Masters title following a famous incident which cost him a play-off place against Bob Goalby. At the 71st hole de Vicenzo had a birdie three; his playing partner, Tommy Aaron, inadvertently marked him down for a four, and de Vicenzo signed for it. The score had to stand and Goalby won the title by one shot. He accepted the decision with dignity, but the event took its toll on him for a while. In 1970 de Vicenzo added a second World Cup individual title to his long list of victories.

When he turned to playing on the Seniors Tour, the de Vicenzo success story simply carried on and he won the 1974 World Seniors title. In 1980 he won the first official US Seniors Championship, and in 1985 he won the Argentine Open for the 16th time – he was 62 and it was 41 years after his first win.

RIGHT: *Roberto de Vicenzo practices before the 1968 British Open at Carnoustie. The Argentinian was the defending champion, having won the title 12 months earlier.*

Bruce Devlin

Born in Australia in 1937, but now living in Texas, Bruce Devlin has been part of the golf scene in the United States since joining the US Tour in 1962.

Before entering the paid ranks, he had enjoyed a notable amateur career. In 1958 he helped Australia to victory over the United States in the inaugural Eisenhower Trophy at St Andrews and a year later he won the Australian Amateur title.

In 1963, when he had been a professional for just one year, he had a memorable season, winning the Australian, New Zealand and French Open titles; the next year he enjoyed the first of his eight US Tour wins when he took the St Petersburg Open. In 1970 he added to his world amateur team title success of 1958 when, along with David Graham, he won the World Cup for Australia, with a record low score of 544. 1972 was Devlin's best year in the States. That was the year of his last Tour win, the USI Classic, when he earned nearly $120,000 to finish eighth on the money list.

In the twilight of his career, when many had forgotten him, Devlin stunned his fellow competitors with opening rounds of 70 and 69 to lead by two at the halfway stage of the 1982 US Open at Pebble Beach. Although he fell away in the final two rounds, he finished a respectable six shots behind winner Tom Watson and reminded the golf world that he was still a force to reckon with.

Today Devlin is regarded as one of the best players of recent times never to have won a major – two fourth placings in the Masters are his best results. Since 1983 he has not played regularly on the Tour. Instead he has been turning his attentions to golf course design and to commentating. In October 1987 Devlin became eligible for the US Seniors Tour.

BELOW: *Australia's Bruce Devlin, identifiable by his very rounded swing. Now living in Texas, he has been part of the US golfing scene for 25 years.*

Leo Diegel

With several close finishes to his credit and regarded today as one of the finest match-play golfers of the interwar era, Leo Diegel's greatest misfortune was that Walter Hagen just happened to be playing golf at the same time as he was.

Born in Michigan in 1899, Diegel was deprived of some of his best golfing years by the First World War. In 1920 he nearly won the US Open at Inverness, Ohio – only a final round 77 cost him the title which went to Britain's Ted Ray instead. Six years later in 1926 he lost to Hagen 5 and 3 in the final of the US PGA Championship at Salisbury, New York. Starting at the first hole after lunch he caused a stir when he shot his ball under Hagen's parked car.

Two years later, however, Diegel's luck improved when he won the first of his two successive PGA titles. After eliminating Hagen, he beat Gene Sarazen 9 and 8 and then beat Al Espinosa 6 and 5 in the final. In 1929 he retained the title by beating the previous year's US Open champion, John Farrell, 6 and 4 in the final. That

same year Diegel won the Canadian Open, the fourth time he had won the title – a record that remains unbeaten today. In 1930 he finished joint second in the British Open at Hoylake, this time beaten by the legendary Bobby Jones who was on his way to his famous Grand Slam.

Diegel had great all-round ability and talent, even though his putting style was unusual – he controlled and powered the club with his elbows. The one aspect of his play that often let him down was nerves: in the 1933 British Open at St Andrews he had an easy putt to tie, but missed by just a foot, so forfeiting the title.

During his 15-year career Diegel won more than 30 tournaments. He was a member of the inaugural US Ryder Cup team in 1927, and played in the 1929, 1931 and 1933 teams too. Leo Diegel died in 1951.

Olin Dutra

ABOVE: *Olin Dutra (right) with Walter Hagen in 1932. The following year Hagen invited Dutra to tour with him.*

One of the best players of the early 1930s, Olin Dutra reached the top through sheer hard work and the dedicated desire to continue improving his game, even after he turned professional.

Born at Monterey in 1901, he used to work in a local store, but got up early three days a week to practice his golf before going to work. Even after turning professional he kept his job to supplement his income, and continued to get up for his early morning practice.

Those years of dedication were rewarded in 1932 when he won the PGA title by beating Frank Walsh 4 and 3 at Keller, Minnesota. The following year he gained Ryder Cup selection but had a disastrous singles, losing 9 and 8 to Abe Mitchell – the second biggest win by a British golfer in the Cup's history. He made amends when selected two years later by beating Alf Padgham 4 and 2 at Ridgewood. Between his two Ryder Cup appearances Dutra won the second major of his career when he came back from an eight-stroke deficit after two rounds to beat Gene Sarazen by one shot to win the 1934 US Open at Merion.

Dutra was highly regarded by the top professional of the day, Walter Hagen, and he was honored by being asked to tour with Hagen in 1933. During his career Dutra won 21 tournaments and was still playing regularly long after he had reached the age of 60, mostly at the Jurupa Hills Club, California, where he was professional. Dutra died in 1983.

Nick Faldo

Since winning the British Youths' Open Championship and then the English Amateur title, eight days after his 18th birthday in 1975, the success story of Nick Faldo simply has not stopped, with 1987 marking a new chapter when he won the British Open at Muirfield. He is certainly regarded as Britain's top golfer today.

Born at Welwyn Garden City in Hertfordshire in 1957, he turned professional the year after his English Amateur triumph. After his first full season on the European Tour he was named 1977 Rookie of the Year after finishing eighth in the Order of Merit. That year he gained the first of his six Ryder Cup selections, and

FAR LEFT: *Nick Faldo, Britain's second Open winner in three years, holds the trophy after the 1987 championship.*

LEFT: *Power is one of Briton Nick Faldo's trademarks.*

at 20 years 59 days became the youngest person to play in the competition.

In 1978 he won his first Tour event when he took the prestigious British PGA Championship, a feat he repeated in 1980 and 1981. Five wins in the 1983 season saw him top £140,000 in prize money and head the Order of Merit. Since 1981 he has also been playing on the US Tour and in 1984 he enjoyed one of the best moments of his career when he became the first Briton since Tony Jacklin to win in the United States when he took the Sea Pines Heritage Classic.

1985 was a disappointing year for Faldo who decided to seek advice in the United States from coach Dave Leadbetter. Leadbetter suggested a change of swing, and during the process Faldo failed to win a tournament in either 1985 or 1986. But in 1987 he came back with a vengeance to win the Spanish Open and then the Open Championship, when he came from three behind Paul Azinger in the final round to snatch victory.

Faldo has vied with Sandy Lyle for the right to the 'Best British Golfer' crown over the past ten years. Although Lyle held this coveted honor temporarily after winning the Open in 1985, in 1987 Faldo had certainly regained his position as Britain's top golfer.

31

Max Faulkner

Halfway through the 1951 British Open at Portrush, Max Faulkner was signing autographs: he was so confident of winning that below his name he was adding 'Open Champion 1951.' His confidence was vindicated when he won by two shots from Argentinian Tony Cerda. Faulkner's victory was to remain the last British success until Tony Jacklin's historic win at the British Open at Lytham in July 1969.

Flamboyant and extrovert, to the point of being eccentric at times, Faulkner was born in Bexhill, Sussex, in 1916. He was instantly recognizable for his brightly colored clothes and the plus-fours for which he became famous. His eccentricity was even more noticeable when one looked inside his golf bag – his collection of clubs not only had different shafts, but different heads and different handles too. Faulkner was constantly changing his clubs – and invariably producing master strokes to win the big tournaments.

Between 1946 and 1968 Faulkner had 16 wins in

ABOVE: *Even in his latter playing days Max Faulkner remained flamboyant, particularly in his choice of brightly colored clothes.*

Europe, including the Spanish Open titles in 1952, 1953 and 1957, the British Professional Match-Play in 1953 and the Dunlop Masters in 1951. He remains the only person to have won the Open, the Match-Play and the Masters titles. Faulkner was selected for the Ryder Cup team five times between 1947 and 1957 (he missed selection in 1955) but, strangely, never won a singles match. In fact, he played in eight matches and only won one, a foursomes with Jim Adams in 1949.

In 1968 Faulkner won the Portuguese Open – at the age of 52. That same year he won the British Seniors title, a feat he repeated in 1970. In recent years Faulkner has enjoyed devoting his time to teaching many up-and-coming British golfers, including Brian Barnes who is married to his daughter Hilary.

Jim Ferrier

Born in New South Wales in 1915, Jim Ferrier became a naturalized American citizen shortly after deciding to try his luck in the United States in 1940.

Originally a sports writer specializing in golf, he began his golfing career as a leading amateur. He won the Australian Amateur title four times and the Australian Open twice, and went on to enjoy a total of 25 wins as an amateur in his homeland.

In 1936 Ferrier came to Britain for the first time and became the first Australian to reach the final of the Amateur Championship, losing by 2 holes to Hector Thompson. It was the first final contested by two men who subsequently turned professional. He was the leading amateur that year, but had to wait until 1944, when he had moved to the States, for his first win as a professional. That first success came at Oakland while Jim was serving in the US Army.

Between the mid-1940s and mid-1950s, Jim Ferrier was one of the game's top earners. His greatest triumph took place in 1947 at Plum Hollow, Michigan, when devastating putting helped him beat Chick Har-bert 2 and 1 in the final of the PGA championship to become the first Australian-born winner of the title – a feat David Graham emulated 32 years later.

In 1950, he stood an excellent chance of achieving his second major. The occasion was the Masters at Augusta and he needed to shoot a 38 on the back nine to win. But at the 13th he found the creek and dropped shots at every remaining hole to finish with a 41, two shots behind Jimmy Demaret. Nevertheless, Ferrier was second to Sam Snead in the money list that year and the following year he won five tournaments, including three successive Tour events. Between 1944 and 1961 he won a total of 21 Tour events.

Very tall, at 6 feet 3 inches, he had a peculiar swing as the result of an accident as a child, which resulted in the dipping of his left knee. What he lacked in driving he certainly made up for with fine putting.

BELOW: *Jim Ferrier lines up a crucial putt during the third round of the 1947 PGA Championship. He won the match and beat Chick Harbert 2 and 1 in the final.*

Dow Finsterwald

Had Dow Finsterwald not been such a cautious player he might well have won more tournaments. Yet in spite of his caution he proved to be one of the most successful golfers on the US Tour during the late 1950s. On two occasions he finished runner-up on the money list, in 1956 and 1958, beaten by Ted Kroll and Arnold Palmer respectively.

Finsterwald was born in Ohio in 1929 and turned professional in 1951. An accurate if cautious player, he experienced a painful moment in that year's Masters when he shot an 11 at the par-three 12th. In 1952 he joined the US Tour and within a few years had scored some notable successes. He was runner-up to Lionel Hebert in the last PGA Championship to be decided over match-play in 1957 and was awarded the Vardon Trophy that year with a stroke average of 70.30. The following year he emerged as US PGA Champion when he shot a final-round 67 to beat Billy Casper by two shots. That was Finsterwald's only major championship success among his 12 Tour wins, although he almost took a second in the 1962 Masters when he was involved in a play-off with such audacious company as Arnold Palmer and Gary Player. Needless to say he finished third, with Palmer taking first place. Between 1957 and 1963 he played in all four Ryder Cup teams and was honored with the nonplaying captaincy at Royal Lytham and St Annes in 1977 when he led the United States team to a five-point win.

RIGHT: *Dow Finsterwald in action in 1962, when he was involved in a three-way play-off for the Masters with Gary Player and Arnold Palmer. Finsterwald took third place, with Palmer taking the title.*

Ray Floyd

RIGHT: *At the age of 43 Ray Floyd defied his years and the pundits who had written him off by winning the 1986 US Open at Shinnecock Hills.*

RIGHT: *At the age of 43 Ray Floyd defied his years and the pundits who had written him off by winning the 1986 US Open at Shinnecock Hills.*

The career of Ray Floyd must surely rank as one of the most surprising in recent years. Twice, when he has apparently been written off by the golfing world, he has responded with brilliant golf.

Toward the end of the 1970s his career looked as though it was at an end. He had slipped to 30th on the rankings in 1978 and had achieved only five Tour wins since the turn of the decade. Then, remarkably, he won the 1979 Greensboro Open and the 1980 Doral-Eastern Open before embarking on what proved to be his two best seasons in 20 years as a professional when he won six Tour events in 1981 and 1982. In each of the two seasons his earnings amounted to more than $350,000 – he was runner-up in the money list to Tom Kite and Craig Stadler respectively.

Included in Ray Floyd's great run was the 1982 PGA Championship, his second PGA title, which came 13 years after his first. He started the tournament with a 63 and led all the way, just as he had done in the 1976 Masters when he had won by eight shots from Ben Crenshaw. Floyd regards that 63 in the 1982 PGA as the finest round of his life.

In 1983 Floyd slipped down the rankings again and the following year was 68th on the money list. Once again the critics wrote him off. Without a win to his name since that 1982 PGA Championship he surprised the golf world by winning the 1985 Houston Open and finishing fifth on the list. In 1986 he defied everybody yet again when he became the oldest winner of the US Open at the age of 43.

Ray Floyd had thus succeeded in winning the championship he felt he needed to complete his career.

35

Ed Furgol

The 17-year professional career record of Ed Furgol is not that impressive; just seven Tour wins, including one major. But he is worthy of inclusion in any list of great golfers because of the way he overcame a tremendous physical disability to challenge the best golfers in the world.

Furgol as a child was involved in a playground accident which left him with a badly withered and almost useless left arm – generally regarded as the more important arm for a golfer's swing. With determination, however, he developed a swing that was virtually all through the right arm, with the left playing a minor role in controlling the club. Despite his disability he could still achieve great distance with his clubs.

A leading amateur during the war years, New York-born Furgol turned professional in 1945. Over the next 12 years he was to become one of the most consistent golfers in the United States. In 1954 he was named PGA Player of the Year largely because of his one-shot win over Gene Littler in the first US Open to be televised, at Baltusrol's lower course. Furgol went on to win the individual title in the World Cup the following year (then known as the Canada Cup), and in 1957 he gained his only Ryder Cup selection – sadly he played in the defeat at Lindrick.

Furgol gave up playing the regular Tour in 1962 at the age of 45. He still played occasionally and a year later tied for fifth place in the Masters, three shots behind the first-time winner Jack Nicklaus.

Al Geiberger

10 June 1977 is a special day in US golfing history. It is also a memorable day in the long career of Al Geiberger. On that day, during the second round of the Danny Thomas-Memphis Classic at the Colonial Country Club, he became the first (and only) man to break 60 in a US Tour event. Two brilliant halves of 30 and 29 contained 11 birdies and one eagle and he only needed his putter 23 times in his 13-under-par round, which he managed to complete with an eight-foot putt on the 18th.

David Graham

The career of Al Geiberger, however, covers more than just that one round of golf. It stretches back 27 years to the time he first played on the Tour in 1960, the year after he made the decision to turn professional.

The 1962 Ontario Open was Al's first Tour win and between then and 1979 he won 11 times on the Tour. His peak years were in the mid-1970s when in 1975 he won the prestigious Tournament of Champions and Tournament Players Championship, in 1976 the Greater Greensboro Open and Western Open, and in 1977 the Danny Thomas-Memphis Classic. In those three seasons alone Al won more than $450,000, a third of his total career earnings.

'Mr 59,' as Geiberger is known for his 1977 triumph, won only one major, the 1966 PGA Championship, by a record four strokes. On two other occasions, in 1969 and 1976, he finished second in the US Open.

Geiberger has been dogged by illness since the 1960s when he was hit with a nervous stomach complaint. That was followed with intestinal surgery in 1978, knee surgery in 1979 and emergency surgery for the removal of his colon in 1980. Had it not been for such bad luck Al Geiberger could well have notched up more notable achievements to add to his record of being the only man to break 60 on the US Tour. As some consolation he ended his first year on the Seniors Tour in 1987 as a leading money winner.

David Graham ranks among Australia's finest golfers. He represents the link between the first great Australians such as Ferrier, Crampton and Devlin, and today's players such as Greg Norman and Rodger Davis.

A fine club designer, Graham turned professional in 1962 and made his way to the States via the Australasian and Asian Tours. En route he teamed up with Bruce Devlin to win the World Cup for Australia in 1970 with a record score of 544. He joined the US Tour in 1971 and in 1983 he overtook Bruce Crampton as the biggest Australian money winner on the Tour.

His first American win was the 1972 Cleveland Open when he beat Bruce Devlin in a play-off. By 1976 he had taken the World Match-Play title at Wentworth and had boosted his US Tour wins to three. Then in the 1979 PGA Championship he recorded a memorable moment. He needed a four at the 72nd hole to win by two shots but he double-bogeyed. In a sudden-death play-off with Ben Crenshaw, he holed putts from 30 feet and 10 feet at the first two extra holes before winning at the next. Then in the US Open two years later he played one of the finest finishing rounds of golf seen in a major championship. When he started the final round he was three shots behind George Burns. But he went on to shoot a final 67 for a seven-under-par 273 – a one-stroke win over Burns and Bill Rogers. In hitting all 18 greens in regulation he had achieved a remarkable feat in Open history.

FAR LEFT: *The smiling Ed Furgol. After severe injuries sustained to his left arm following a childhood accident, his achievements as a golfer seem all the more remarkable.*

LEFT: *'Mr 59,' Al Geiberger, in action during the 1975 World Match-Play final at Wentworth. Fellow American, Hale Irwin won the match 4 and 2.*

RIGHT: *David and Maureen Graham in jubilant mood after David had beaten the defending champion, Hale Irwin at the 38th hole to win the 1976 World Match-Play title at Wentworth.*

Hubert Green

Since breaking into the top 30 on the US Tour in 1971, his second season on Tour, Hubert Green has been one of the biggest names in world golf.

Born in 1946 in Birmingham, Alabama, he was the youngest of four children and followed in the footsteps of his brother and two sisters, all of whom played golf. As they lived near the Birmingham Country Club this was an inevitable starting place for the Green golfers.

During his time at the Florida State University, Hubert's game developed considerably, although his amateur career was not outstanding. He turned professional in 1970 and came through the Tour qualifying school that fall. His first Tour win, which was to be the first of 19 US wins for Green, was his first Tour event, the 1971 Houston Open. In the mid-1970s Green was constantly in the top 10 and in 1977 he won the first of his two majors when he took the US Open at Southern Hills, Tulsa. He showed true determination that day – not only did he manage to sink a pressure putt from three feet at the 18th and so win by one from Lou Graham, but he did so with an anonymous assassination threat hanging over his head.

A bad shoulder injury caused him to drop to 135th on the rankings in 1983, but surgery, the Green grit and hard work helped him to get back among the elite. In 1985 he won the PGA Championship at Cherry Hills when he beat off a challenge from Lee Trevino for one of golf's most popular wins. His winnings that day took him past the $2 million mark, as he became the 14th man in golfing history to reach that milestone.

LEFT: *During the 1970s Hubert Green was one of the most consistent golfers in the United States.*

Ralph Guldahl

In four brief years at the top, Ralph Guldahl, who was born in Dallas in 1911, made a lasting impression on the American golfing scene.

He first attracted attention in the 1933 US Open when he stood a good chance of forcing a tie with amateur Jimmy Goodman, but missed a four-foot putt at the 72nd hole. Little was heard of Guldahl after that as he was rarely seen on the US Tour, but in 1936 he returned, and with a vengeance, winning the Western Open – regarded as highly as the majors at that time. In 1937 he not only retained his title, but also won his first major and narrowly missed a second.

In the Masters that year victory was in sight when he stood on the 12th tee in the final round. Byron Nelson was the man most likely to catch Guldahl and over the next two holes he gained six shots on Ralph with a 2 and a 3 compared to Guldahl's 5 and 6. That disappointment was forgotten a couple of months later when Guldahl won the US Open at Oakland, beating Sam Snead, playing in his first Open, by two shots and with a championship record 281 that stood until beaten

ABOVE: *Ralph Guldahl (right) receiving the US Open trophy in 1937 from second-placed Sam Snead after Guldahl had won by two strokes at Oakland Hills.*

by Ben Hogan in 1948.

Guldahl's success continued when, in 1938, he became the first and only man to win the Western Open in three consecutive years. He tied second place in the Masters, behind winner Harry Picard. The pattern of repeated victories continued further when he won the US Open for a second time to become the fourth player in history to win the event back-to-back. After twice coming close in the Masters, Ralph eventually won the title in 1939, when a 33 on the back nine gave him the title by one stroke from Sam Snead who had looked a certain winner at the start of the last 18 holes.

Shortly after playing in the 1940 US Open at Canterbury, Ohio, Ralph Guldahl quit tournament golf in order to concentrate on his club professional's job in Chicago and to spend more time with his family.

Walter Hagen

Professional golfers owe a great debt to Walter Hagen, golf's first superstar, for the tremendous amount he did to raise the status of the profession of golf.

Walter Hagen's unorthodox approach to the game made him the most extrovert and flamboyant character in the history of the sport. A great leg-puller and crowd pleaser, he was also a great sportsman.

Born and bred in Rochester, New York, he came from a poor background and used to earn money caddying at the local golf course. He later became an assistant at Rochester, and in no time was attracting a lot of attention as a good golfer. It was not long before the word 'good' was being replaced by 'great.'

Walter Hagen was a superb putter, but his carefree approach was probably his greatest asset. While fellow competitors were at home worrying about the next day's play, Hagen was out on the town enjoying an affluent lifestyle. He once arrived at a tournament still dressed in a tuxedo from the previous night's binge!

Hagen was the first of the great American-born golfers to dominate world golf and he was joined in the 1920s, in a golden era of American golf, by Bobby Jones and Gene Sarazen. Together the three were responsible for the US invasion of the British Open Championship and for winning the title eight times between 1922 and 1932. Hagen won the title at St George's in 1922 to become the first American-born winner of the title; then again at Hoylake in 1924 and once again in 1928 with a back-to-back win at St George's. In 1929 he achieved another back-to-back win at Muirfield when he had a fine six-stroke win over a strong field containing the US Ryder Cup team.

Harold Hilton

Hagen's dominance of professional golf had started in 1914 when he won the US Open at Midlothian, Illinois, after leading for all four rounds. In 1919 he beat Mike Brady in a play-off for the title, but it was in the PGA Championship that he showed his skill as the leading match-play golfer of the era. In 1921 he won the first of five titles. He did not compete in 1922, lost at the 38th to Gene Sarazen in 1923 and then went 22 consecutive matches without defeat during which time he won four consecutive titles. The PGA Championship remains the only US PGA event won four years in succession by one man.

With 11 major championships behind him, Walter Hagen died in 1969 at the age of 76.

ABOVE: *The very relaxed Harold Hilton.*

Along with John Ball, Harold Horsfall Hilton was the outstanding British amateur golfer at the turn of the century. Coincidentally, both golfers came from the same part of England, the Wirral, and both played for the Royal Liverpool club at Hoylake. By a further co-incidence, Hilton was born in 1869, the year of the formation of the Royal Liverpool club.

Appropriately Hilton was the winner of the first British Open, played at Hoylake in 1897, when a great final round 75 was enough to beat James Braid by one shot. Hilton had also won Muirfield's first championship five years earlier when he beat Ball, Hugh Kirkaldy and Alex Herd by three strokes. Between them, Hilton and Ball dominated the Amateur Championship at that time, with a total of 12 wins.

Hilton won his first title in 1900, after three defeats in the final, when he beat James Robb 8 and 7. He retained his title in 1901 and when he won in 1911 he completed a rare double, becoming the first man to win the US and British Amateur titles in the same year. Only Bobby Jones, Lawson Little and Bob Dickson have emulated the feat. In 1913, 22 years after first appearing in the final, Hilton beat Robert Harris at St Andrews to win his fourth British Amateur title.

Although he was only 5 feet 7 inches tall, his power belied his size and made him a giant of British golf in the days of such great professionals as Braid, Taylor and Vardon. He later wrote several authoritative books on the game, and in 1911 became the first editor of *Golf Monthly*. He died in 1942 at the age of 73.

Ben Hogan

Ben Hogan is a golfing legend. No other word can suitably describe the greatest golfer of the immediate postwar years. And remarkably, some of his greatest triumphs came after he cheated death in a horrific car accident.

Returning to their Fort Worth home in 1949, Hogan and his wife Valerie were involved in a car accident with a truck. In an act of instinctive bravery Hogan threw himself across his wife. The accident left him with multiple injuries and he was, at one time, given up for dead. Doctors told him he would never walk again, let alone play golf . . . But eleven months later he was contesting the Los Angeles Open.

Then, in June 1950, 16 months after the accident, he won the 50th US Open, once again defying medical reckoning. His win came after he had played 36 holes on the final day to force a three-way 18-hole play-off with Lloyd Mangrum and George Fazio. Hogan won by four strokes. His success, on a tide of national emotion, is one of the sport's great romantic stories.

Born in Dublin, Texas, in 1912, Hogan turned professional in 1931. Along with Sam Snead and Byron Nelson he formed golf's second 'Great Triumvirate' after Vardon, Braid and Taylor. Between them, the threesome won 200 US Tour events; Hogan's total of 62 is third only to Snead and Jack Nicklaus. They also won 21 majors, but Hogan held the best record of the three, with nine wins to his credit.

Surprisingly, the man with the perfect golf swing had to wait seven years before his first win as a professional, the 1938 Hershey Fourball. His next win took place in 1940, and between 1940 and 1942 he was top of the money list. It was after the war years, however, that his record was truly outstanding.

In 1946 he won the US PGA and over the next three seasons he won 31 tournaments, including the 1948 US Open at Riviera with a record 276. His accident put him out of action in 1949 but then he had that remarkable win at Merion. He retained his US Open title in 1951 and added the first of two Masters titles that year.

But his greatest year was to come when, in 1953, he won the Masters, the US Open and the British Open, to become the first man to win three majors in one year. Hogan regarded his 1953 Masters win as one of the best of his career because his rounds of 70, 69, 66 and 69 were to stand as a record for 12 years. When he won the US Open that year he was to join Bobby Jones and Willie Anderson as the only four-times winners of the title. His win at Carnoustie was just as celebrated. Hogan had been reluctant to make the trip for his one and only British Open because he disliked traveling after his accident. But persuaded by friends he made the trip and his four-stroke win proved immensely popular with the British public. Had the 1953 PGA Championship not clashed with the British Open, Hogan might well have become the first man to win all four titles in one year.

Ben Hogan was a man of few words who tended to shun adulation. He felt he was there to do a job and should not be praised for doing it. His golf was clinical and consistent, his preparation thorough. Between 1940 and 1956 he played in 30 majors, achieving 22 top-five finishes. Not even Jack Nicklaus could claim such a level of consistency.

Hogan should have retired after his great 1953 season but he still had a burning desire to compete and win. When he shot a third round 66 in the 1967 Masters, at the age of 54, people began conjuring up nostalgic visions of his past performances. He only succeeded in achieving joint 10th place, but this was enough to remind people that Ben Hogan was still a tough and keen competitor.

LEFT: *Ben Hogan practicing for the 1956 Canada Cup at Wentworth. Representing the USA, Hogan and Sam Snead won the title by 14 shots.*
RIGHT: *The usually poker-faced Hogan can raise a smile, but he can only just raise the PGA Trophy which he won in 1948 after beating Mike Turnesa.*

Jock Hutchison

Along with Jim Barnes and Walter Hagen, Jock Hutchison ranks as one of the dominant figures in US golf in the period before the arrival of Bobby Jones.

Born in St Andrews in 1884, Jock was in his teens when he and his family moved to the United States and settled in Pittsburgh.

In 1916 he scored a notable success when he came close to achieving an impressive double – after finishing second to Charles Evans in the US Open, he was beaten by just one hole in the Inaugural USA PGA Championship by Jim Barnes. Four years later, in 1920, he won the coveted Western Open (a title he regained in 1923), and came second once again in the US Open. Later that year he eventually won his first major when he beat J Douglas Edgar by one hole to win the PGA at Flossmoor, Illinois. In 1921 he visited the town of his birth, St Andrews, where he delighted a vast army of fans with some of the best approach play to the greens ever seen at that time. In successive holes he achieved a hole-in-one and a two, only inches away from a second hole-in-one. Three shots for two consecutive holes is still a British Open record. In spite of these scoring feats, Britain's Roger Wethered chased him all the way and forced a 36-hole play-off which Hutchison won by nine shots making him the first man to take the famous trophy to the United States.

Hutchison gave up championship golf in 1928, but returned in 1941 with the start of PGA Seniors golf, winning the Seniors Championship in 1947. In 1959 he was elected to the PGA's Hall of Fame.

LEFT: *Scottish-born American Jock Hutchison during the 1922 Open at Sandwich. A year earlier he had become the first American to win the title with his success at his hometown of St Andrews.*

Hale Irwin

In Hale Irwin you have a brilliant shotmaker, a great stylist and a man with tremendous competitive spirit. With these ingredients the recipe can only spell success – which is precisely what Irwin has enjoyed in his 20 years on the professional circuit.

Consistency has been the key to his achievements over the years, and from early 1975 to the end of the 1978 Tour he went 86 tournaments without missing a cut, the third best streak ever on the Tour.

A former NCAA champion, the bespectacled Irwin turned professional and joined the US Tour in 1968. His first win was the 1971 Heritage Classic, which he won again two years later, but Irwin's first big year was 1974 when he surprised the golf world by winning the US Open at Winged Foot, beating another up-and-coming youngster, Forrest Fezler, by two shots. Irwin took the World Match-Play crown at Wentworth later in the year and he retained that title in 1975. Only

ABOVE: *The bespectacled Hale Irwin has been a leading member of the US Tour for nearly 20 years. This picture was taken in 1977.*

defeat by David Graham at the 38th hole in 1976 prevented a hat-trick of wins.

1979 was another outstanding year in Irwin's career. He won his second Open Championship, at Inverness, Ohio; despite a final round of 75 he managed to beat Jerry Pate and Gary Player by two shots. Nearly two years later Irwin won the 1981 Hawaiian Open. After working on a new swing, he then went on to register a win every year until 1986 when he slipped out of the top 50 for the first time since 1969.

In 1987, however, he succeeded in taking the Florida Invitational, reminding people never to write him off. He is still playing today with the same youthful determination first seen on golf courses 20 years ago.

Tony Jacklin

Ask any sportsman to describe the highlight of his career and he will give an instant answer. But ask Tony Jacklin that question, and he'll reel off three answers.

Undoubtedly the first great moment in his long career was at Lytham in 1969 when he beat left-hander Bob Charles to take the British Open title and become the first Briton for 18 years to lift the coveted trophy. Jacklin cherished another great moment in 1985 when he led the European team to victory in the Ryder Cup at the Belfry, thereby inflicting defeat upon the United States team for the first time in 28 years. Then two years later he captained the first visiting team to win the Cup on American soil.

Much respected within the game, Jacklin is the son of a Lincolnshire steel-worker. Jacklin himself started his working life as a steel-worker's apprentice before becoming assistant professional to Bill Shankland at Potters Bar in Hertfordshire in 1961. He was only 17 at the time, but had succeeded in getting his foot on the first rung of the ladder.

He turned professional in 1962 and in 1965 won his first big tournament when he was the Assistant Pro-

ABOVE: *Tony Jacklin blasts the ball out of the bunker during the 1969 British Open at Lytham.*
LEFT: *Jacklin in action in the same Open.*
RIGHT: *Jacklin in 1985 as captain of the first British Ryder Cup team in 28 years to beat the American team.*

fessionals' champion. In 1967 he won the Pringle tournament and the prestigious Dunlop Masters, his first wins on the European Tour.

In 1968 Jacklin decided to try his luck in the United States. He soon proved his standing as a world-class golfer by becoming the first Briton to win on the US Tour when he took the Jacksonville Open title. That was followed in 1969 by his British Open win and less than a year later he became the first Briton since Ted Ray in 1920 to win the US Open. If anyone wanted further proof that Tony Jacklin was one of the world's greatest golfers at the time they had only to look at his performance at the Open at Hazeltine – Jacklin beat Dave Hill by seven strokes, the biggest winning margin for 49 years; he was the only player to beat par; and

Don January

to cap this achievement, he led from start to finish.

Jacklin's exploits during those 12 months brought about a renewed interest in golf in Britain and many young people took to the sport, inspired by Jacklin's successes. Another assault on America in 1972 brought him a second Jacksonville Open title and in 1982 he won his last European event, the Sun Alliance PGA Championship at Hillside, Southport.

Since then Tony's skills as a leader have been all too evident in his captaincy of the Ryder Cup team. He first held this honor in 1983 and came close to doing something which had never been achieved before – winning in the United States – but the home team scraped home by one point. Two years later Jacklin put the record straight with a great win at the Belfry and then in 1987 he led the side to a fine win at Muirfield Village, Ohio. His own playing record in the Ryder Cup was impressive and he played in seven successive competitions from 1967 to 1981.

For the important contribution Jacklin has made to golf he was made an honorary member of the British PGA, and was awarded the OBE.

ABOVE: *Don January, a successful member of the Seniors Tour.*

Don January joined the US Tour in 1956. Today, more than 30 years later, he is still playing consistently good golf as a member of the US Seniors Tour.

His first win on the regular Tour took place in his Rookie Year when he won the Dallas Open. Five years later in 1961 he came very close to winning the PGA Championship at Olympia Fields, Illinois. In the play-off he shot a 68, but Jerry Barber shot a 67 to take the title. In 1967 January eventually won his one and only major championship, the PGA at Columbine, when he beat Don Massengale by two shots in a play-off.

For a short period from 1972 to 1975 January turned his attention to course design, but to boost his income he returned to the regular Tour and in 1976 won the last of his 11 Tour wins, taking the prestigious Tournament of Champions event. He tied in second place in the PGA that same year and finished ninth on the money list with a personal best of $163,622. The following year January gained his second Ryder Cup selection and became, at 47 years 300 days, the oldest American ever to play in the series.

January surpassed the $1 million career earnings total in 1979 and in that same year he joined the Seniors Tour. Since becoming a Senior he has won more than 20 tournaments. In 1987 he completed a unique double when he became the first man to win the Tournament of Champions on the regular Tour and then go on to win the Seniors Tournament of Champions.

Bobby Jones

When he retired from competitive golf at the age of 28 in 1930 Bobby Jones was able to look back on one of the most remarkable records in the history of golf.

An amateur throughout his career, he won 13 majors, a record that remained until beaten by Jack Nicklaus. Bobby Jones also held the unique record of winning the amateur championships of Britain and the United States, as well as the Open championships of both countries, all within a single year, 1930.

Born in Atlanta, Georgia, in 1902, Jones graduated from college with engineering, law and literature degrees. It was to law that Jones turned, building up a successful legal practice in Augusta. Because of his business interests he chose to reject lucrative offers to turn professional and to remain an amateur instead. In spite of his amateur status Bobby Jones was regarded as the greatest golfer of his era, if not of all time. And, at a time when the professional ranks were rife with

talent like Gene Sarazen and Walter Hagen, Jones emerged as the leading player of the 1920s.

Jones started playing golf at the age of five and soon realized the importance of a good swing. He went on to develop a swing that was full and fluent, involving a complete 90-degree turn of his hips. His complete mastery of his swing enabled him not only to get to but to stay at the top of the game.

For someone whose senior career lasted only from 1923 to 1930 Bobby Jones's list of achievements seems all the more impressive. He won his first major in 1923 when he took the US Open after a play-off with Bobby Cruickshank at Inwood. Next he won the first of five US Amateur championships in 1924, retaining the title a year later. His remarkable run went on to include the British and US Open titles in 1926 and another double in 1927 with the British Open and US Amateur titles. The US Amateur followed again in 1928 but in 1929

ABOVE: *Bobby Jones (left) with his great rival Walter Hagen (right), competing in the Masters Invitational Tournament at Augusta in 1934.*
LEFT: *Bobby Jones seen in the Open at Hoylake during his 'Grand Slam' year, 1930.*

Jones completed his first barren year since 1922. In 1930 he more than made up for the previous year's performance when he completed golf's most remarkable 'Grand Slam' by winning four major championships within a single year.

This outstanding year in his career got off to an auspicious start when on 31 May he beat Britain's Roger Wethered 7 and 6 to win the British Amateur title at St Andrews. Less than a month later he won the British Open at Hoylake when he beat fellow American Leo Diegel by two strokes. Next he won the US Open, also by two strokes, from Macdonald Smith at Interlachen. Then, on 27 September, record crowds flocked to see whether Jones could pull off golf's greatest feat by

completing the Grand Slam. He did, with an easy 8 and 7 victory over Eugene Homans in the US Amateur at Merion – on the same course that he had won his first US Amateur title in 1924.

Having achieved this ultimate accolade in his golfing career Bobby Jones retired shortly afterward to concentrate on his legal practice. He was not lost to golf altogether, however, because he went on to make a series of instructional films. He was also largely responsible for the inauguration of the US Masters in 1934. Although he played in the event every year from its beginning until 1946, the competitive edge had gone from his game.

In the 1950s Jones learned he was suffering from a spinal disease. He still made the trip to St Andrews in 1958 for the first Eisenhower Trophy match where he was given the freedom of the Burgh of St Andrews in recognition of his 1930 triumph. In the end Jones became paralysed in his arms and his legs and he died with dignity at Augusta in 1971.

Tom Kite

If you measure success by the number of major championship wins then Tom Kite has been a failure. But if you measure success by consistency, then Tom Kite is undoubtedly one of the best golfers.

His career includes a number of near misses – he finished joint second in the British Open at St Andrews in 1978 and twice finished joint second in the Masters at Augusta, in 1983 and 1986. In 1986 he needed an 11-footer at the last to force a tie with Jack Nicklaus – but he missed. In spite of all these near misses Tom Kite has been an outstanding golfer since he turned professional in 1972.

Born in Texas in 1949 he showed early promise, emerging as a star junior player. He started playing golf at six and by 11 had won his first tournament. He was runner-up to Lanny Wadkins in the 1970 US Amateur Championship. In 1971 Walker Cup honors followed and the next year he shared the NCAA title with Texas teammate Ben Crenshaw.

In 1973 Kite was named Rookie of the Year, with winnings of $54,270. Three years later he won his first tournament when he took the IVB-Bicentennial Golf Classic. The Tom Kite success story, however, only really began in 1981.

That year he won only one tournament, but in 26 starts he scored an amazing 21 top-ten finishes to head the money list. He was also awarded the Vardon Trophy that season with a stroke average of 69.80 per round – one of ten occasions his average has been under 70. The following year he retained the Vardon Trophy finishing third on the money list. He missed the cut just once in 25 starts and when he did, in the Canadian Open, it happened after he had completed a run of 53 successive tournaments.

Since 1981 Tom Kite has won a tournament every year. Among the other regular players currently on the Tour only such great names as Jack Nicklaus, Lee Trevino and Hubert Green have been able to match Kite's level of consistency. But Kite can claim the distinction of being the only man to have won on the Tour every year since 1981.

Although his win in the 1987 Kemper Open was only the 10th Tour win of his career Kite has nevertheless won a total of over $3 million (the fourth best of all time) – an indication of how consistent a player he is.

LEFT: *Tom Kite is now the fourth biggest money winner of all time. In 15 years he has won more than $3 million on the US Tour, but he would swap a large part of that for just one major.*

RIGHT: *Bernhard Langer, the greatest player to come from West Germany, has in recent years challenged Seve Ballesteros for the coveted position of top European golfer.*

Bernhard Langer

Bernhard Langer has emerged from a nation that plays little golf to become not only one of the finest golfers in Europe but one of the best in the world. He has proved his outstanding ability by taking on American adversaries in their own 'back yard' . . . and beating them. His record of back-to-back US victories in 1985 is further proof of his rise to the top of the golfing tree.

Born in West Germany in 1957 Langer is, without doubt, the best golfer the country has produced and his rise to the top is the result of sheer hard work. When he was 15 he left school and went to Munich to work as an assistant professional. At 18 he joined the European Tour, but failed to finish higher than 40th on the Order of Merit in his first four seasons. In 1979 he won the coveted Cacherel Under-25s Championship by a massive 17 strokes and the following year all his hard work paid off when he achieved his first European Tour win, the highly regarded Dunlop Masters.

Since then Bernhard has been a consistent winner and has twice, in 1981 and 1984, topped the European Order of Merit. In 1984 he attacked the US circuit and has since been a regular Tour member. His first US win was in the 1985 Masters when two closing rounds of 68-68 gave him the title by two strokes from Seve Ballesteros, Curtis Strange and Ray Floyd. A week later Langer stamped his authority on the Tour with victory in the Sea Pines Heritage Classic. A great year ended when Langer played a vital role in Europe's win over the United States in the Ryder Cup.

Langer continues to win tournaments worldwide on both the US and European circuits. A powerful hitter and a master of approach shots to the green, Langer has been let down over the years by his putting which tends to be too tense at times. But when his putting is at its best Bernhard Langer is without doubt a world beater of truly outstanding ability.

Tony Lema

It takes a lot of audacity for a golfer to come to St Andrews for his first tournament over the famous Scottish course and then expect to win without a practice round. But that is precisely what 'Champagne' Tony Lema did in 1964, when he won the British Open, beating the great Jack Nicklaus by five strokes.

Although he had been professional since 1955, and winning tournaments since 1957 when he won the Imperial Valley Open, it was only in the 1960s that he started to attract attention as a top-class player.

Well known for the showbusiness lifestyle he led, Tony Lema was given his nickname when he promised champagne to journalists if he won the 1962 Orange County California Open. He won and duly kept his word. Thereafter he was dubbed 'Champagne' Tony. In his first Masters in 1963 he nearly had the audacity to win; only a 20-foot putt from Jack Nicklaus at the 72nd deprived him of victory. But he certainly made amends at St Andrews a year later when he won the Open on his first attempt. One of golf's great and most

dramatic matches followed in England in 1965. Lema was leading Gary Player by seven shots with 16 holes to play in the semifinal of the World Match-Play Championship at Wentworth, but Player, the match-play expert, achieved victory at the 37th. That same season Lema was runner-up to Nicklaus on the US money list with $101,000, making him the third man after Nicklaus and Palmer to win over $100,000 in a season.

That, sadly, was to be his last year on the Tour because in 1966 on his way back from a PGA event in Akron, the plane he was traveling in crashed on a golf course at Lansing, Illinois. The crew, Lema and Lema's wife Betty were killed instantly. Golf had lost one of its great players who might well have gone on to greater things had he lived. He was only 32.

BELOW: *Tony Lema (center) waiting for Britain's Neil Coles to tee off during their match in the first World Match-Play Championship in 1964. Coles won their match and went on to play Arnold Palmer in the final.*

Lawson Little

ABOVE: *Lawson Little proudly holds the trophy after winning the British Amateur title for the second successive year in 1935 at Lytham.*

Lawson Little shares with the legendary Bobby Jones the distinction of winning the US Open, the US Amateur and the British Amateur titles. But Little stands alone as the only man to win the amateur titles of *both* countries in successive years.

A semifinalist in the US Amateur in 1933, he won his first major event the following year, the year of his first Walker Cup selection, when he took the British Amateur at Prestwick, beating local hero Jack Wallace 14 and 13, still a record score for the final. He emulated Bobby Jones by adding US titles in the same year, but in 1935 he went one better than Jones by retaining both titles. He beat Bill Tweddell by one hole to win the British title at Lytham and at the Country Club, Brookline, he beat Walter Emery 4 and 2. In 31 consecutive matches in the two tournaments, he didn't ever lose. In 1936 Little turned professional and a win in the Canadian Open that year suggested his professional career would prove as successful as his amateur career. But this was not to be, although Little did enjoy one moment of glory in 1940 when he beat Gene Sarazen in a play-off to win the US Open held that year at Canterbury, Cleveland.

In 1961, in recognition of his outstanding amateur record, Lawson Little was admitted to the PGA Hall of Fame. He died in 1968 at the age of 57.

Gene Littler

Likeable Gene Littler can pride himself on a career which stretches back to the 1950s. He was born in San Diego in 1930, and his career got off to an impressive start when he won the US Amateur title in 1953. The following year he won his first US Tour event, the San Diego Open, while still an amateur. That year he turned professional and finished second to Ed Furgol in the Open at Baltusrol. Littler then entered the record books by becoming the only golfer to win the Tournament of Champions three years in succession (in 1955, 1956 and 1957).

Five Tour wins in 1959 put him second on the money list behind Art Wall, but he had still failed to win a major. This was put right in 1961 when he won the US Open at Oakland Hills, thanks to a final-round 68 which gave him a one-stroke win. That year he gained the first of seven Ryder Cup selections.

Littler came close to taking the 1970 Masters, but in the play-off against Billy Casper he lost by five shots. Two years later Littler had to undergo surgery for cancer, and, for the first time in his 19 years as a professional, he had finished outside the top 35. Fortunately he recovered and winning ways soon returned; in 1974 he became the eighth man to surpass $1 million in career earnings.

In 1977, 23 years after coming close to winning the US Open, he came close to winning his second major championship. Littler was 47 at the time. With nine holes remaining he led by five shots and looked certain to win the first PGA Championship at Pebble Beach. But Lanny Wadkins forced a play-off and won at the third extra hole. Littler's 29th and last US Tour win took place the same year, when he won the Houston Open. His total of 29 might have been greater had it not been for illness and his poor play-off record – he won only three of 11 such confrontations. As it was, Gene Littler had a long and successful career. His total of wins is the 12th best of all time on the US Tour. Had he converted half those near misses into wins he would comfortably be among the top ten golfers of all time.

Littler went on to join the US Seniors Tour in 1980. His career was interrupted when, in 1984, he broke his left arm. He had to have pins inserted and these were not removed until 1987. Nevertheless, this setback failed to impair Littler's appetite for the game and in 1987 he won more than $60,000.

At his home at Rancho Santa Fe, California, Gene Littler enjoys spending time with his wife Shirley – and his collection of vintage cars.

RIGHT: *Gene Littler in action during the 1976 British Open at Birkdale. Despite his many successes, Littler never managed to do well in this Open.*

Bobby Locke

with the golfing authorities, he returned to the British and European circuits.

In 1949 he won the first of four British Open titles when he beat Harry Bradshaw in a play-off at Sandwich. He retained the title a year later at Troon and in 1952 embarked on a period of great rivalry with Australian Peter Thomson, with Locke winning at Lytham. Thomson then dominated the Open until Locke won for the fourth time, at St Andrews in 1957, with Thomson runner-up.

Locke won more than 80 tournaments worldwide, but returned to his native Transvaal for his final tournament win, the 1958 Transvaal Open. A car crash in 1960 left Locke's eyesight impaired and he played little serious golf after that. His difficulties continued after his playing days – he was given a three-month suspended prison sentence for manslaughter following the shooting of a man who had demanded money from him. Arthur D'Arcy 'Bobby' Locke, one of the world's best putters, died in 1987 after a brief illness. He was 69.

LEFT: *The amiable South African Bobby Locke after winning his first British Open title in 1949.*
BELOW: *Locke (left) wearing the plus-fours and white cap that were his trademarks, and Syd Scott in 1952.*

A hickory-shafted putter, along with dark blue plus-fours, a white cap and dashing white shoes, became the trademarks of the likeable South African golfer, Bobby Locke. The skill with which he handled his putter placed him in the same league as the greats Walter Hagen and Bobby Jones as a master of putting.

Born in the Transvaal in 1917, he was only eight when he played off a handicap of 14. Before he turned 18 he won the South African Open title as an amateur. He was still an amateur when he won the title again in 1937. By the following year, however, he had turned professional and won the same title again. Altogether he was the South African Open champion nine times between 1935 and 1955.

During the war he served as a bomber pilot with the South African Air Force which meant a two-and-a-half-year layoff from golf. When he returned to the game in 1946 he headed for Britain. For some years Walter Hagen had been trying to persuade him to play in the States and in 1947 he eventually made the trip. After a poor opening, notably in the Masters, he took the US Tour by storm, winning seven tournaments, including four in five starts. His impressive performance placed him second on the money list to Jimmy Demaret.

Locke returned in 1948 and continued to play outstanding golf. His victory by 16 strokes in the Chicago Victory National remains a US Tour record. After a brief stay in the States where he found himself clashing

Liang-Huan Lu

Born in Taipei in 1936 and known affectionately as 'Mr Lu,' Liang-Huan Lu was the youngest ever winner on the Asian circuit when he won the 1959 Hong Kong Open at the age of 22. He became a regular winner on the Far Eastern golf circuits, taking many Open titles.

In 1971 during the British Open at Birkdale he enthralled golf fans in an exciting battle with 'Super Mex' himself, Lee Trevino. His habit of doffing his trilby every time the crowd acknowledged him became his trademark. Lu trailed Trevino in the opening round by just one stroke. But from then on the two players matched each other round-for-round. That opening round cost Lu the title.

The week after his British Open 'triumph' he gained consolation by winning the French Open at Biarritz with a championship record 262 – at the time, the joint second lowest score ever achieved on the European Tour. But perhaps the greatest moment of Mr Lu's long career came in 1972 when, with Hsieh Min Nan, he helped Taiwan to a surprise victory in the World Cup in Australia. In 1974, he finished joint fifth in the British Open at Lytham, his second best result in the championship. Since then he has spent most of the time playing on the Asian circuit, winning most of their major tournaments. He also devotes much of his time to his hotel business in Taiwan.

RIGHT: *Taiwan's 'Mr Lu' upstaged Lee Trevino in the popularity stakes during their classic encounter in the 1971 British Open at Royal Birkdale.*

Sandy Lyle

When your father is a golf professional, the chances are you will follow in his footsteps. Sandy Lyle did not upset any odds.

His father Alex became professional at Hawkstone Park, Shropshire in 1955, three years before Sandy was born. When he was three the Lyle youngster picked up his first golf club and hit the ball a staggering 80 yards. Naturally his father gave him plenty of encouragement, even though Sandy was equally fond of soccer at the time.

By the time he was 14 Sandy was a junior international; at 17 he won the 1975 English Amateur Stroke-Play Championship, a title he won for a second time two years later. In 1977 he won Walker Cup honors and within two years had been selected for the Ryder Cup team, a feat only previously achieved by Mark James, in 1975 and 1977.

In 1977 Sandy turned professional, his first win coming in the 1978 Nigerian Open on the Safari Tour. With an amazing round of 61 he served notice of what lay in store for the golf world. Lyle was already being tipped as a future star.

These predictions have certainly proved accurate. Along with Nick Faldo, he has formed one half of Britain's outstanding golfing duo of the 1980s. Lyle is one of the most powerful men in the game, utilizing his large 6-foot 1-inch frame to the full. He is one of the longest drivers and his long-iron play is superb. Not only has Sandy proved a great competitor and winner on the European circuit but he has proved he can conquer the tough world of the US Tour and he has done something only one other Briton (Tony Jacklin) has achieved – won twice on the Tour. In 1986 he won the Greater Greensboro Open and in 1987 took the Tournament Players Championship at Sawgrass after beating Jeff Sluman in a play-off.

Highly regarded and respected both sides of the Atlantic, Sandy certainly showed he was a true champion when he won the coveted British Open title at St George's in 1985 to become the first Briton since Tony Jacklin, 16 years earlier, to hold the famous trophy aloft. Lyle opened well with a 68, tying for second place with Australian David Graham, but four behind Christy O'Connor Junior. At the halfway stage Graham and Lyle led on 139. Then Lyle fell away with a 73 and it looked as though it would be a two-horse race between Graham and the new challenger Bernhard Langer. But Lyle's grit saw him shoot a level par 70 while the two leaders both returned 75s – Lyle won by one from the American challenger Payne Stewart.

RIGHT: *One of the longest hitters currently playing on the European circuit, Sandy Lyle has emerged as a world class golfer in recent years.*

John McDermott

John McDermott's fall from the top of world golf was as dramatic as his rise to the top.

As an 18-year-old he lost the three-way play-off, involving the Smith brothers, Alex (the eventual winner) and Macdonald, in the 1910 US Open at Philadelphia. Twelve months later he *won* a three-way play-off, beating Mike Brady and George Simpson at Chicago to win the title, and at 19 years 10 months and 14 days, become the youngest winner of a major tournament this century, and the second youngest of all time.

McDermott retained the title in 1912 with a two-stroke win over Tom McNamara, and in 1913 he won the Shawnee Open by a massive seven strokes from Britain's best of the day, Harry Vardon and Ted Ray. To complete a memorable year, he won the Western Open and Philadelphia Open, finished joint fifth in the British Open, and ninth in the US Open. Although he won the North and South Open in 1914 this was to be his last season. The pressure of emerging as a world beater in such a short period had taken its toll and in 1915 he suffered a nervous breakdown.

When he died in 1971 at the age of 80, this master of backspin had left his mark on golfing history. He may have been at the top for only four or five years but he was the youngest winner of the US Open, as well as the first home-bred winner of the great championship.

RIGHT: *When he won the US Open at Chicago in 1911 John McDermott became the youngest winner of a major championship this century, an honor he still holds today.*

John Mahaffey

RIGHT: *Texan John Mahaffey – on a good day he is one of the best strikers of the ball.*

When he is striking the ball well no golfer can touch John Mahaffey. Unlike most young golfers in the United States who concentrate on their drive when they first turn professional, he has worked on accuracy instead.

An outstanding college player, he won the NCAA title for the University of Texas in 1970 and turned professional the following year. His first Tour win was in the Sahara Invitational in 1973 but he was still an unknown when he tied the 1975 US Open with another unknown, Lou Graham, at Medinah. Graham won the play-off by two strokes.

During the 1976 PGA Championship at the Congres-sional Mahaffey developed elbow trouble, which turned out to be a hyperextended tendon, and he lost a big part of the 1977 season. He came back with a bang in 1978 and won his second Tour event, the PGA Championship held at Oakmont.

In the 1986 Tournament Players Championship at Sawgrass he snatched victory from under Larry Mize's nose when Mize led by three with four to play. It is fair to say that Mize 'threw' his opportunity away, but only consistent play by Mahaffey, and in particular with his putter, allowed him to be in there at the 'death.' Mahaffey took first prize and helped boost his career earnings to over $2 million in 1986.

Lloyd Mangrum

The Second World War deprived Lloyd Mangrum of three years on the US Tour. Had he not lost those years, between 1943 and 1946, he would surely have achieved more than 34 Tour wins by the end of his career. As it was, his total is the eighth best of all time.

Lloyd Mangrum was born in Texas in 1914 and followed his brother Ray into the world of professional golf. Lloyd turned professional in 1938 and enjoyed his first win that year when he took the Pennsylvania Open. In the 1940 Masters he shot a first round 64, a record for any major at that time, and a Masters record that was not equaled until 1965 when it took a player as great as Jack Nicklaus to do so. Mangrum had to be

satisfied with finishing runner-up to Jimmy Demaret, in spite of his excellent opening round.

Just as he was reaching the top World War II broke out and he was taken away from golf. For his heroic wartime service Mangrum was awarded two Purple Hearts. And appropriately when he was wounded in action he was sent to St Andrews to recuperate. Once the war was over he took up his golf clubs again. In the 1946 US Open he was involved in a three-way tie with Byron Nelson and Vic Ghezzi. All three shot 72s in the first play-off round; then Nelson and Ghezzi each shot 73, while Mangrum shot 72 to take the title.

For the next ten years Mangrum played consistently well in the States, winning eight Tour events in 1948. He was also a regular member of the Ryder Cup team, with notable singles wins over Britain's best – Max Faulkner, Fred Daly and Harry Weetman. In the 1949 Masters Mangrum was runner-up to Sam Snead. The following year he was once again involved in a three-way play-off for the US Open title. This time he was the loser to Hogan who destroyed Mangrum and George Fazio in the play-off. In 1951 Mangrum came top of the money list and was awarded the Vardon Trophy for the lowest stroke average, a trophy he won again two years later.

This cool successful player, who was constantly seen with a cigarette in his mouth, slipped down from his position at the top in the mid-1950s, the same time as his great rival Ben Hogan started his decline. Mangrum was inducted into the Hall of Fame in 1964 and died in 1973, at the age of 59.

ABOVE LEFT: *Lloyd Mangrum, captain of the winning Ryder Cup team at Wentworth in 1953, proudly holds the trophy.*

LEFT: *Lloyd Mangrum teeing off against Henry Cotton in the 1949 News of the World Tournament at Walton Heath in Surrey, England.*

FACING PAGE, LEFT: *Jubilation for Dave Marr as he birdies at the 15th at Laurel Valley.*

FACING PAGE, RIGHT: *Forty-five-year-old Arnaud Massy during the 1922 Open at Sandwich.*

Dave Marr   Arnaud Massy

Although Dave Marr cannot claim a startling number of successes, he is a much respected man in his various capacities in the golfing world as player, journalist and television commentator.

The likeable Texan turned professional in 1953 at the age of 20, but did not join the Tour for seven years. In his Rookie year he won the Sam Snead Festival and from then on won money every year for the next 17 years. He came close to winning the 1964 Masters when he tied with Nicklaus for joint second place, six shots behind Arnold Palmer.

In 1965, however, Dave Marr became the PGA Champion when he won by two strokes from Jack Nicklaus and Billy Casper at Laurel Valley. In winning the title, Marr had emulated the feat of his cousin Jack Burke who had won the title nine years earlier. Although Marr was the PGA Player of the Year in 1965, that PGA win was the last of four Tour wins he was to enjoy. He gained Ryder Cup selection at the end of the year and in 1981 he was nonplaying captain of the team, again emulating his cousin, who had captained the side in 1973.

In recent years Marr has been cutting down on his tournament appearances. The man with a good swing and good short-game has served on the US PGA Championship committee and was at one time chairman. In 1984 Dave Marr returned to competitive golf when he joined the USA Seniors Tour.

Frenchman Arnaud Massy holds a special place in British Open history as the first continental winner of the championship. It took 72 years and Severiano Ballesteros for the record to be repeated.

Massy first competed in the Open at Hoylake in 1902, when he was 25. He tied for 12th place, 17 shots behind the winner, Sandy Herd. Massy decided to stay in Britain and took a job as a club maker with Ben Sayers at North Berwick. After the 1905 Open, when he finished fifth at St Andrews, he returned to France to take up the position of professional at La Boulie. He won the first French Open in 1906 over his 'home' course and retained the title in 1907 when he beat James Braid, again at La Boulie.

That year he came to England for the Open at Hoylake, scene of his first Open five years earlier. But this time it was a better result as he challenged the monopoly of the 'Great Triumvirate' by beating J H Taylor by two strokes. With this win Massy became the first foreigner to win the British Open. During this Open one of his daughters was born and he named her 'Hoylake' to commemorate the event.

Powerfully built and with a delicate putting touch, Massy was very popular amongst his fellow professionals. With his fine record of achievement on the course he can deservedly be considered the first great European champion. In 1910 he became the first winner of the Belgian Open. In 1911 he came close to his second Open but lost the play-off to Harry Vardon when he conceded at the 35th extra hole as his position was hopeless. The following year he became the first winner of the Spanish Open. He competed in his last British Open in 1922, at the age of 45 . . . three years later he won his fourth French Open and in 1928 he won the Spanish Open at the amazing age of 51! When Massy died in 1958 he was 81 years old.

Cary Middlecoff

Cary Middlecoff waited until he had completed his training as a dentist before turning professional. He was 26 years old at the time and had an outstanding amateur record behind him. Middlecoff thought it would be wise to have a career to fall back on if he failed to make it in the golf world. His caution proved unnecessary as he was destined to become one of the top professionals in the United States in the 1950s.

He first served notice of his golfing ability in 1945 when he became the first, and only, amateur to win the prestigious North and South Open. When he turned professional he won the Charlotte Open, his third professional tournament. From then on he remained a regular winner until 1961.

A slow, often frustratingly slow, player, he used to take a long time adjusting himself for each shot, but his actions were justified by the results – three major wins and runner-up on four occasions.

In the 1948 Masters he finished second to club professional Claude Harmon but then won the US Open at Medinah a year later with Sam Snead and Clayton Haefner in pursuit. 1955 proved an outstanding year

for 'The Doc,' as Middlecoff was known. He won five Tour events, including the Masters when he beat Ben Hogan by a record seven strokes. On his way to the title he holed a putt reputedly over 80 feet long at the large 13th green.

That year he was beaten into second place by the great putting of Doug Ford in the PGA Championship at Meadowbrook, Detroit. But he achieved his third major a year later when he won the US Open from Hogan and Julius Boros and in 1957 he came close to his third Open title when he holed a 10-footer to force a play-off with Dick Mayer at Inverness, Ohio; 'The Doc' lost the play-off by seven shots. In 1959 Middlecoff finished second again, this time in the Masters; Art Wall had five birdies in six holes to win by one.

Back trouble and the dreaded putting twitch, 'the Yips,' brought an end to Middlecoff's career in 1961. He left the Tour with 37 wins behind him, the seventh best record of all time. During his career he also won the Vardon Trophy in 1956 and played for the United States in three Ryder Cup matches in 1953, 1955 and 1959. In 1974 he was elected to the PGA Hall of Fame.

LEFT: *Dr Cary Middlecoff gave up dentistry to become a professional golfer. His record shows he made the right decision.*

RIGHT: *The 'Golden Boy' of American golf in the early 1970s, Johnny Miller. In 1974 he toppled Nicklaus as the biggest money winner in the United States.*

Johnny Miller

In 1966 Johnny Miller went to the Olympic Club in his native San Francisco to caddy in the US Open. He was barely 19 at the time and took part in the pre-qualifying tournament. He qualified and finished eighth. That was the first sign that a superstar was about to burst onto the golfing scene. Johnny Miller did just that between 1973 and 1976 when he joined Jack Nicklaus as one of the world's two outstanding golfers.

A devout Mormon, Miller has been deeply religious all his life. As a golfer he was already being hailed as 'the next Jack Nicklaus' in 1971. Johnny Miller was a great striker of the ball; when he shot a final round 63 for victory in the 1973 US Open he served notice that he had arrived. Strangely, among his 23 US Tour wins, this was to be his only US major.

Miller threatened Nicklaus in the early part of the 1970s and in 1974 toppled the great man as the leading US money winner after a three-year spell on top. Miller's total of $353,021 was more than $100,000 higher than Nicklaus's, and came about when he won eight Tour events, a figure bettered by only three men, and all giants of the game – Snead, Hogan and Nelson. Between 1974 and 1976 Miller won a staggering 14 US Tour events; Nicklaus won nine. Miller also successfully outplayed Nicklaus and the up-and-coming youngster Seve Ballesteros to win the 1976 British Open at Birkdale by six shots.

In the late 1970s Miller's game began to slip. One reason was his desire to spend more time away from the golf course, and enjoy time with his wife Linda and their six children. Two other reasons were the fact that he had lost his desire to succeed – success had taken that out of him. He was also having problems with his swing, which undermined his confidence. He put his game back together, physically and mentally, and started winning again in the 1980 Inverrary Classic and went through the next four seasons with a tournament win each year. He achieved his 20th Tour win in the 1981 Los Angeles Open and in 1984 Johnny Miller took his career earnings past $2 million.

Larry Mize

Larry Mize arrived on the US Tour in 1982. He finished 124th on the money list that year. Since then his progress has been rapid and he has never finished lower than 36th. His first Tour victory, the Danny Thomas-Memphis Classic, came in 1983. When his second win came, it could not have been in more dramatic style.

It was in the 1987 Masters at Augusta, Mize's home town, and he fulfilled his childhood dream by winning the coveted title. What is more, he had to beat some very distinguished company before taking the title, and placing himself among golf's elite. In the final day of play he emerged as an unknown to challenge Greg Norman and Seve Ballesteros for the lead. His final round 71 forced a sudden death play-off. The Spaniard fell at the first extra hole and at the next Mize played a majestic chip shot from 140 feet which went in the hole for a birdie, giving him victory.

Larry started playing golf at the age of nine under the guidance of his father, a scratch golfer. His amateur career was of little note, but when he joined the US Tour in 1982 his classic swing and overall style were likened to Tom Watson's in his younger days. With his rapid rate of progress it seems certain that a promising future lies ahead for Larry Mize.

Orville Moody

Which golfer turned professional at the age of 33, spent 15 years on the US Tour, and won only one event – the US Open in his second year? The answer is Orville Moody. Despite this seemingly abysmal record, Moody has been a key part of US golf since turning professional in 1967.

Moody was uncertain whether he wanted to turn professional, but decided to undergo a two-year trial period. He was on the verge of quitting the Tour when he emerged as the surprise winner of the Open in 1969. The success persuaded Moody to continue playing, and today he is still part of the US golfing scene as a member of the Seniors Tour.

An Oklahoman and part Choctaw Indian, he spent 14 years in the army where he was placed in charge of maintenance and instruction at the army's golf courses. During his time in the forces, he won the All-Army Championship in 1958, and the All-Services Championship in 1962.

He came out of the army in 1967, to go on to the Tour's qualifying school the same year. His first season as a pro proved disastrous. He was 103rd on the money list with less than $13,000. But if that year was a write-off, 1969 was an impressive triumph. He jumped to 21st position on the money list, thanks to his win in the Open when he won by one shot from Deane Beman, Al Geiberger, and Bob Rosburg at the Champions Club, Houston. Moody's close friend Lee Trevino predicted before the Open that if he (Trevino) didn't win the title then Moody would. Moody teamed up with Trevino to win the World Cup for the United States later in the year, and was voted PGA Player of the Year in 1969. That great season could have been even better had he not lost the play-off to Gene Littler in the Greater Greensboro Open. Orville never enjoyed another season like that. His next best season was in 1973 when he finished 36th on the money list with winnings of $74,286. His best result of the season was in finishing second to Jack Nicklaus, after a play-off, in the Bing Crosby.

In the 1980s he curtailed regular Tour events to join the Seniors Tour in December 1983. In his Rookie year he won two official events and one unofficial event, and in 1987 he won more than $100,000 on the Tour – something he had never achieved on the regular Tour.

LEFT: *Larry Mize lines up a putt. It was not the putt that won him the 1987 Masters in his hometown of Augusta but a 140-foot chip shot instead.*

RIGHT: *Orville Moody became a professional golfer at the age of 33. He nearly quit after two years, but changed his mind after winning the US Open in 1969.*

Tom Morris Senior & Junior

Tom Morris Senior

Born at St Andrews in 1821, 'Old Tom' Morris was one of the first true greats of the game. He was narrowly beaten by Willie Park in the first British Open held at Prestwick in 1860, but over the next seven years he was to win the title no less than four times.

In 1861 he beat Willie Park by four shots to win his first title. A year later he beat Park to retain his title with a margin of 13 strokes – still an Open record. After finishing second to Park in 1863 Morris won for the third time the following year.

The year after his third win, Morris returned to St Andrews to become the head greenkeeper at the Royal and Ancient, a post he held until 1904, when he was 83. In 1867 he won the Open for a fourth time, before being succeeded as champion by his son, Tom Junior, who was to become the best golfer of the era. When he won his fourth title, at Prestwick, 'Old Tom,' so called to distinguish him from his son, was 46 years 99 days old and he remains the oldest winner of the title. He went on to play in every British Open championship from 1860 to 1896, when he was 75 years of age.

Morris began playing golf at the age of six and at 15 was an apprentice ball-maker to Allan Robertson. He

BELOW: *'Old Tom' (left) and 'Young Tom' Morris.*

and his employer started teaming up to play pairs challenge matches. One such match, for the then large sum of £400, was against Willie and Jamie Dunn of Musselburgh. Robertson and Morris came from being four down, with eight to play, to snatch victory in the third and deciding match. After severing his connection with Robertson, Morris became a club and ball maker on his own for the three years before he moved to Prestwick.

After falling down the stairs at the St Andrews clubhouse in 1908 'Old Tom' Morris, one of the first golfing legends, died at the age of 87.

Tom Morris Junior

Without doubt, 'Young Tom' Morris was the greatest golfer in the early days of championship golf. And for someone who was only 24 when he died, his achievements seem all the more remarkable.

He played in his first Open in 1867 at the age of 16, finishing fourth. A year later he won the title – the start of three consecutive wins. At the time he was only 17 years 5 months old, and he is, to this day, the youngest winner of the title. He is also credited with the first ever hole-in-one in the Open; that was at Prestwick's 166-yard eighth hole in 1868. After his third Open win Morris was allowed to keep the leather Championship Belt. Because a trophy was not available in 1871 there was no British Open. When the Open was revived in 1872 Morris became the first winner of the new trophy, the magnificent claret jug which is still the most sought-after prize in golf today.

Morris was the first true tournament player, as opposed to a working professional, and his dominance of the sport between 1868 and 1875 was total. This was never more obvious than in his third Open win in 1870 when he covered Prestwick's 36 holes in 149, winning by 12 strokes. Low scoring like that had never been seen before and it was not until 1904 that the championship was won with a better average score.

While playing a pairs match with his father against Willie and Mungo Park at North Berwick in September 1875, 'Young Tom' received a telegram saying his pregnant wife was seriously ill. He boarded a boat and sped back to his St Andrews home. But it was too late – his wife and newborn baby had died. Tom started drinking heavily after that and died on Christmas Day at the age of 24. As a measure of respect 60 golfing societies around Britain contributed to the erection of a memorial in the cemetery at St Andrews Cathedral.

Kel Nagle

One of the most popular golfers among fans and fellow professionals alike, Australia's Kel Nagle was late coming into the professional ranks. Born in Sydney in 1920 he took an assistant's job just before the war but had to wait until 1946 when the hostilities were over before turning professional. In 1949 he won the Australian Professional Championship, but achieved little of note for the next five years until 1954 when he was Peter Thomson's partner in the winning Australian Canada Cup (now World Cup) team.

Nagle spent several years developing his short game and in 1957 he started a great run of success that saw him emerge as one of the most consistent golfers over the next ten years. He won the New Zealand Open in 1957 and in 1958 and a year later added the Australian Open. But the high point in his career came at St Andrews in 1960 when he won the Centenary British Open title by one shot from the strong challenge of Arnold Palmer who was playing his first Open. A second Open was there for the taking two years later. Nagle was a strong contender at the halfway stage, but Palmer responded with a six-stroke win.

The US Tour was Nagle's next target and in 1964 he became the oldest winner of the Canadian Open at 43 years of age. He nearly added the US Open to his list of titles the following year but he lost the play-off to South Africa's Gary Player by three shots.

A regular on the British and Asian circuits, as well as in the United States, Nagle continued winning in Australasia and in 1969, one month before his 49th birthday, he won his seventh New Zealand Open. A new chapter in the life story of Kel Nagle was written in 1971 when he beat Julius Boros to win the World Seniors title – a win as popular as ever.

RIGHT: *Popular Australian golfer Kel Nagle on his way home after winning the centenary British Open at St Andrews in 1960.*

'Tommy' Nakajima

'Disaster' should be 'Tommy' Nakajima's middle name. Although he is Japan's leading golfer, along with Isao Aoki, he has never won a major championship since turning professional in 1975. He has come close a couple of times, only to be deprived by a disaster of one sort or another.

A three-month spell in 1978 will linger in Nakajima's memory for years to come. Firstly, in the Masters at Augusta he played into a bunker at the 13th – and completed the hole in 13 shots. Then in the British Open at St Andrews three months later he bunkered at the infamous Road Hole when in contention with the leaders. By the time he eventually got out of the sand he was out of contention, having taken a nine!

In the 1986 British Open at Turnberry Nakajima met with further bad luck when he challenged Australian Greg Norman. Nakajima was in with a realistic chance of becoming the first Japanese golfer to win a major when he started the final round. He was one behind Norman – but three-putted from six feet at the first

hole. From then on he allowed his game to slip away and he finished down the field in eighth position, nine shots off the lead. That year he was also engaged in a memorable match with Britain's Sandy Lyle in the Suntory World Match-Play Championship at Wentworth before Lyle won at the second extra hole.

'Tommy' (his real name is Tsuneyaki) has not always been a loser. He won the Japanese Amateur title in 1973 and, after turning professional, has won the Japan PGA title three times, in 1977, 1983 and 1984, and the Japan Open twice. He is second to Aoki as the all-time money winner on the Asian circuit, and in 1986 he was the first Japanese golfer to win over 100 million yen in one season. Nakajima has been less successful on the US circuit – he has never managed to break into the top 50 money winners.

BELOW: *'Tommy' Nakajima getting out of a bunker. On two memorable occasions bunker shots have proved disastrous for the Japanese golfer.*

Byron Nelson

In 1944 and 1945 Byron Nelson won 26 US Tour events. Many sports writers were stinting in their praise, saying a lot of the good golfers of the day were away performing military service (Nelson was exempt because he was a haemophiliac). These remarks were ill-founded when you consider Sam Snead provided much of Nelson's opposition. And when you look further at his amazing run between March and August 1945 when he won 11 consecutive events, a figure that still stands today and will probably continue to stand for all time, there is little doubt about the magnitude of Byron Nelson's achievements. His 18 wins in 1945 is also a record that should last forever.

Nelson was born in Fort Worth, Texas, and turned professional at the age of 20, in 1932. At first he was not particularly successful and had to wait three years for his first win, the New Jersey Open. Two years later he served notice that he was ready to take the Tour by storm: at Augusta in 1937 he gained six shots on Ralph Guldahl in the final round to win the Masters.

He took his second major in 1939 when he won a three-way play-off against Craig Wood and Denny Shute in the US Open. Later in the year he was runner-up in the PGA Championship to Henry Picard, but the following year took the title when he beat Sam Snead by one shot in the final. He was runner-up again in 1941 and was also second in that year's Masters, to Craig Wood. But it was back to winning ways in 1942 when he engaged in a great battle with Ben Hogan in the Masters, before winning by one shot.

Nelson appeared in his fourth PGA final in six years in 1944 but was the loser for the third time. The tables were turned a year later when he appeared in his fifth final to beat Sam Byrd 4 and 3. In the 1946 US Open, he was once again the loser, this time to Lloyd Mangrum who finished first ahead of Nelson and Vic Ghezzi after a play-off. The following year Nelson had to be content with another second place, behind Jimmy Demaret in the Masters.

Although he didn't manage to come close to a major again, Nelson continued winning on the US Tour up to 1951 and ended his career with 54 Tour wins to his credit. At the peak of his career during the war years, he went 113 consecutive tournaments without missing a cut, thus adding further fuel to his claims that his great run in 1944 and 1945 was entirely due to the standard of his play, not the quality of the opposition. Only Snead, Nicklaus, Hogan and Palmer have won more Tour events than Nelson. To finish fifth behind those great names is an achievement in itself.

Larry Nelson

Hitting your first golf shot at the age of 22 and then, 12 years later, winning your first major is quite an achievement. But that is what Larry Nelson did, adding a second major two years after his first!

Born in Alabama in 1947, he toyed with the idea of becoming a baseball or basketball player. He attended college for a year and went on to do military service, during which time he served in Vietnam. He was still undecided about his future when one day in 1969 he went to a golf driving range – the bug hit him and he knew he wanted to become a professional golfer.

He turned professional within two years and in 1973 joined the US Tour, but had to wait six years for his first win, in the Inverrary Classic. He also won the Western Open the same year and finished second to Tom Watson on the money list.

When he won his first major, the PGA Championship in 1981, it was appropriate that it should be on his hometown course at the Atlanta Athletic Club. He beat Fuzzy Zoeller by four shots that day. Two years later he only had one stroke to spare as he beat Tom Watson in the US Open at Oakmont. The one stroke came at the 16th in the final round when he sank a monster putt from over 60 feet to seal his victory.

A born-again Christian, Nelson tends to spend a lot of his time away from the golf course, particularly with his family, and his game has suffered as a result. After the 1984 Walt Disney World Classic he failed to win until 1987 when he surprised the golf world by beating Lanny Wadkins in a play-off to earn his second PGA title and a place in his third Ryder Cup team. He went on to win the Walt Disney World Classic and take his season's winnings to over $400,000.

BELOW: *A deeply religious man, Larry Nelson won his second PGA title in 1987.*

Jack Newton

The golf world was horrified in 1983 when Australian Jack Newton was involved in a tragic accident when he walked into the propeller of a Cessna aircraft at Sydney's Mascot airport. For weeks his life was in danger. Thankfully he was saved, but he had lost the sight in his right eye and lost his right arm. Despite these disabilities Jack Newton was back on a golf course 12 months later. And within two years of the accident his handicap was under 18.

Such determination stems from Newton's schooldays when he played cricket and rugby union with enormous competitive spirit. It was only a rugby accident that forced Jack to take up an alternative sport – golf. He turned professional in 1971 and played on the European Tour, enjoying success in the Dutch Open and Benson & Hedges International at Fulford the following year.

Apart from the accident at Sydney, the most heartbreaking moment of Jack Newton's career was at Carnoustie in 1975 when he lost the play-off for the British

ABOVE: *Jack Newton (left) holding the British Open trophy with Tom Watson before their 18-hole play-off at Carnoustie in 1975. Watson went on to win his first title by one stroke.*

Open by one stroke to Tom Watson. A bit of luck on Watson's part, and a collapse by Newton when he was leading by two shots with four to play in the final round, led to the play-off. The two golfers remained neck-and-neck for most of the 18 deciding holes, but Watson chipped in for an eagle at the 13th and then Newton put his shot to the 18th into the bunker. Watson had won the title.

Newton went on to join the US Tour in 1977, staying for six years. During this period he only once finished in the top 60 of the money list, and he won just one tournament, the 1978 Buick Open. Newton then returned to play the European, Asian, African and Australasian circuits before his tragic accident brought his competitive playing days to an end.

Jack Nicklaus

It is all too easy to describe a sportsman or woman as the 'greatest'. But in describing Jack Nicklaus it is impossible to think of any other suitable word to convey his stature in the world of golf. He has been, and still is, one of *the* greatest golfers of all time. His influence on golfers the world over has been immense.

Nicklaus emerged on the professional golfing scene in 1962 unlike anyone before him. The US Amateur Champion in 1959 and 1961, he was also the NCAA champion in the second of those years and had appeared on two winning US Walker Cup teams. He also helped the United States to a record 42-stroke winning margin in the 1960 Eisenhower Trophy.

His enormous talent was talked about across America and there were few, if any, who doubted his ability to survive in the world of competitive professional golf. He had already proved himself in the 1960 Open at Cherry Hills when, as an amateur, he pushed the great Arnold Palmer all the way before losing by two shots to Palmer's final round 65. In 1962 he joined the US Tour and his first win was the US Open that year at Oakmont, when he beat Palmer by three shots in a play-off. Jack Nicklaus had arrived.

It is difficult to condense Jack Nicklaus's achievements into a short space. But among his many accomplishments are: top money winner eight times between 1964 and 1976, and never out of the top four between 1962 and 1978; PGA Player of the Year five times between 1967 and 1976; member of six Ryder Cup teams between 1969 and 1981, as nonplaying captain in 1983 and 1987; member of six World Cup winning teams 1963-73; winner of six Australian Open titles between 1964 and 1978; winner on the US Tour 71 times, runner-up a staggering 58 times. He has also

ABOVE: *Jack Nicklaus's first success in the British Open was in 1966 at Muirfield. The win had such a special place in his heart that he named his own course in Columbus after Muirfield.*

LEFT: *Nicklaus during one of his early visits to Britain, for the 1959 Amateur Championship at Sandwich.*

RIGHT: *There is no mistaking the Jack Nicklaus style.*

won a record 18 professional majors: the US Open in 1962, 1967, 1972 and 1980; the British Open in 1966, 1970 and 1978; the US PGA in 1963, 1971, 1973, 1975 and 1980; the US Masters in 1963, 1965, 1966, 1972, 1975 and 1986.

Singling out highlights from such an impressive list is even more difficult. But there are two events that gave Jack great personal pride and pleasure, the 1983 Ryder Cup and the 1986 Masters at Augusta. For Nicklaus the captaincy of the Ryder Cup team was in itself an honor; and he was delighted when his team won by the narrowest of margins, thus preventing the first ever US defeat on home soil. Four years later he had the dubious distinction of being the first US captain to lose the Cup on home soil. Winning the 1986 Masters, his sixth Masters win, was especially gratifying because he came through a tough field of young determined players, as well as experienced men like Greg Norman and Seve Ballesteros, to take the title that has been

ABOVE: *Jack Nicklaus with son Jacky . . . could Jacky be another golfing superstar in the making?*

synonymous with his name for 20 years. At the age of 46 he could pride himself on becoming the oldest golfer to wear the famous green jacket.

Nicklaus has given back to golf as much as he has derived from the game. He has been responsible for the design of many fine golf courses all over the world – the Muirfield Village Club is one example – and it was over 'his' course that the 1987 Ryder Cup was played.

In recognition of his enormous contribution to golf, Nicklaus was awarded the US Athlete of the Decade Award 1970-79 in 1980. Today, more than 25 years after his first major win, he is still feared whenever he participates in a tournament. His son Jacky is developing into a fine player, and if he follows in his father's footsteps, golf could find itself dominated by yet another Nicklaus for the *next* 25 years.

Greg Norman

When Greg Norman started out on the long road that has taken him to the top of world golf, his coach Charlie Erp told him not to think too much about accuracy, but to make sure he hit the ball long off the tee. Accuracy, said Erp, would follow, and his philosophy proved right. Norman is now one of the most formidable hitters on a golf course and one of the most lethal and successful golfers of recent times.

Born in Queensland in 1955, he is the latest in a long line of top Australians to dominate the European and American golf circuits. Norman was 16 when he first took up golf, but within two years he was a scratch golfer. In 1976 he turned professional and won the Australian West Lakes Classic that year. His first European win was the 1977 Martini International, which he retained the following year. In 1977 he played in America for the first time in the Memorial Tournament. By 1982, when Greg was the top European money winner after wins in the prestigious Dunlop Masters, the Benson & Hedges International and the State Express Classic, he had gained a reputation for being a globetrotter and had won tournaments in his home country, Europe, Japan, Hong Kong and Fiji.

He was ready to attack the US Tour and in his first official season on the Tour finished ninth on the money list with wins in the Kemper and Canadian Opens. 1985 proved a disappointing year for Norman both in the United States and in Europe, where he failed to win a tournament, although he won three tournaments back home in Australia. But ahead of him lay what would prove the greatest year of his career.

In 1986 he enjoyed outstanding success, winning the Las Vegas Invitational and the Kemper Open to emerge the top money winner in the United States, with a record $653,296. In Europe he won the British Open at Turnberry, the European Open and the Suntory World Match-Play Championship at Wentworth – £224,373 in total, and second only to Ballesteros, who played the Tour regularly all season. Norman returned to Australia and won three tournaments in a row.

In contrast, the following year was comparatively barren for the 'Great White Shark,' so nicknamed because of his blond hair, and the supposed stories that he used to kill sharks when a youngster in Queensland.

His staggering winnings in 1986 could have been increased substantially had he not 'collapsed' in the final round of the three majors that he did not win. Although he led as he went into the final round of all four major championships, he only managed to win one, the British Open. No man has won all four in one season, but Greg Norman certainly came close to re-writing the record books in 1986.

LEFT: *Greg Norman has plenty to smile about. He knows he has the 1986 British Open in hand and that he will at last be the winner of a major.*

OVERLEAF: *There is a definite killer instinct about Norman's expression – it is no surprise he is known as the 'Great White Shark.'*

Christy O'Connor

When he paid his second visit to England, to compete in the Swallow-Penfold Tournament at Southport in 1955, Irishman Christy O'Connor returned home with the first ever check for £1000 in British golf. Fifteen years later he won the John Player Classic to collect the first check for £25,000 in British golf. It is hardly surprising, therefore, to learn that Christy O'Connor was one of the biggest money winners in European golf during that period.

Christy O'Connor was one of the most consistent performers in Europe for more than 25 years, and between 1955 and 1973 he appeared in a record 10 British Ryder Cup teams. With Harry Bradshaw, he also helped Ireland to win the World Cup in 1958, and he represented Ireland 15 times in that competition.

A tremendously gifted player with a beautifully synchronized swing, O'Connor, known as 'Himself,' started life as a caddie in his hometown of Galway, before turning professional in 1951 at the age of 27. He became professional at Royal Dublin in 1959 and among his many fine achievements are the 1957 PGA Match-Play Championship and the 1956 and 1959 Dunlop Masters titles. Between 1955 and 1972 he won 24 European tournaments. In 1961 he played at Royal Birkdale, finishing joint third behind Arnold Palmer in the Open, and in 1965, at the same venue, he was runner-up to Peter Thomson. In the 1982 Carrolls Irish Open at Portmarnock he finished joint third – an impressive achievement as he was 57 years old.

Still a regular in Seniors golf, he has won the World Seniors title twice, in 1976 and 1977, and he has taken the British title six times between 1976 and 1983. His nephew, Christy Junior, is currently a member of the European PGA Tour.

BELOW: *'Himself' Christy O'Connor, Ireland's finest golfer of the 1950s and 1960s. His nephew Christy Junior is also a very fine tournament professional.*

Peter Oosterhuis

Just as the performance of Tony Jacklin, Britain's leading golfer, was beginning to slip, along came Peter Oosterhuis, young, fresh and ready to step in as Britain's number-one player.

He had the right credentials. He had been the British Youths' Champion in 1966 and had represented his country in the 1967 Walker Cup and in the Eisenhower Trophy a year later.

At 6 foot 5 inches, Oosterhuis often looks uncomfortable when lining up a shot, but for such a tall man he has a delicate touch around the green. His early days as a professional were spent in South Africa. When he finished seventh in the Order of Merit on the European Tour in 1970, his promise was clearly evident. Over the next four years he was to replace Tony Jacklin as the top British player when, as winner of the Order of Merit, he was awarded the Vardon Trophy four years in succession. Only Severiano Ballesteros has subsequently won the trophy four times. Between 1971 and 1981 Oosterhuis was selected for the Ryder Cup team every year and it was not until 1979 that he was beaten in the singles by Hubert Green at White Sulphur Springs.

For two years in succession, in 1973 and 1974, he was voted the Golf Writers' Player of the Year; only one other person had won the trophy in successive years, and that was Jacklin in 1969 and 1970. Oosterhuis's performance in the 1973 US Masters had been impressive. At 24 he became the youngest foreign player to lead the tournament, three strokes ahead of his nearest rival, but a disastrous final round 74, to Jesse Snead's 70 and Tommy Aaron's 68, saw him finish in third place. The following year at Royal Lytham he finished runner-up to Gary Player in the Open, four strokes behind the South African. Eight years later he was runner-up to Tom Watson at Troon.

After his near-triumph in the 1973 Masters Oosterhuis realized that if he was to be among the golfing elite he would have to play on the US Tour, so he joined the following year. He settled in California and began playing mainly in the United States. His greatest triumph came when he became the first Briton since Jacklin to win on the Tour, taking the Canadian Open title by one shot from Jack Nicklaus, Bruce Lietzke and Andy North in 1981. That season he finished 28th on the money list but then slid down the rankings to 188th in 1986, thus forfeiting his Tour card. Oosterhuis continued playing the Mini-Tour but, because of his popularity, he received invitations to compete in several of the major Tour events too.

LEFT: *Britain's Peter Oosterhuis deserted the European Tour in the 1970s to try his luck on the tough US Tour where he has enjoyed notable success.*

Francis Ouimet

When 20-year-old amateur Francis Ouimet decided to enter the 1913 US Open because it was taking place locally, at the Brookline Country Club over the road from his home, he could hardly have imagined he was about to change the course of golfing history.

The cream of the British golfers were at Brookline, including Harry Vardon and Ted Ray, who were among the world's top golfers at the time. However, Ouimet played superbly; he went into a three-way play-off with Vardon and Ray and 18 holes later emerged as the victor, five shots ahead of Vardon. His win was to mark the end of British dominance in golf, and the start of American superiority through such men as Walter Hagen and Bobby Jones.

Ouimet followed this success by winning the US Amateur title a year later when he beat defending champion Jerry Travers 6 and 5. He lost the Amateur final to Chick Evans in 1920 but in 1931, and a record 17 years after his first win, he won his second title, beat-ing Jack Westland 6 and 5. Significantly, his second win came the year after the retirement of Bobby Jones who had dominated the amateur scene in the 1920s.

Ouimet, who never turned professional, helped form the backbone of the US Walker Cup team. He played in a record eight matches. In 1932 he succeeded Jones as captain and led the side six times.

One of the original 12 members of the PGA's Hall of Fame in 1940, his achievements were honored in 1951 when he became the first American captain of the Royal and Ancient. He died in 1967 at the age of 74, leaving a unique legacy – ever since that day at Brookline in 1913 American golfers have, apart from the odd hiccup, dominated world golf.

BELOW: *Francis Ouimet, the US captain, practicing for the 1938 Walker Cup. Twenty-five years earlier he changed the face of US golf by winning the US Open despite opposition from the top Britons of the day.*

Arnold Palmer

Perhaps more than any other golfer Arnold Palmer has helped to popularize the sport and to promote and improve the image of the game.

Palmer showed how much fun golf could be. As a result, kids all over the United States and Britain took up the sport. His approach and attitude to the game made it look easy and enjoyable. Palmer was also largely responsible for encouraging fellow American professionals to make the trip to the British Open in the early 1960s. In the postwar years Americans had tended to ignore the event thereby undermining its credibility, but Palmer played his part in reviving its standing as a truly international event.

Palmer's most important role in raising the status of the game came when he teamed up with the top marketing man Mark McCormack. Together they promoted the sport using the powerful medium of television. Sponsors were soon attracted and they, in turn, brought big money into golf.

Born in Latrobe, Pennsylvania in 1929 Palmer turned professional in 1954, shortly after winning the Amateur Championship. The following year, his first year on the Tour, he won the Canadian Open. From that date on until 1973, when he won the Bob Hope Desert Classic, he was to amass a grand total of 61 Tour event wins. Today he ranks fourth in the line-up of the greatest golfers of all time, behind Sam Snead, Jack Nicklaus and Ben Hogan.

Palmer's list of wins includes seven majors – the Masters four times, the British Open twice and the US Open once. That sole US Open win in 1960 was after one of the most remarkable collapses in golfing history, when leader Mike Souchak went into the fourth round seven shots ahead of Palmer. Palmer scored a remarkable final round 65, to Souchak's 75, thus taking the title by two shots from his pursuer, the amateur Jack Nicklaus.

Six years later Palmer was party to another memorable turnaround in US Open history. At the Olympic Club, California, Palmer led Billy Casper by seven shots with nine holes to play. Then disaster struck and at the end of 72 holes they were all square; Casper went on to win the 36-hole play-off by four shots.

Palmer continued to be a top-ten money winner up to 1971, when he finished third. From then on his performance declined rapidly as he competed against talented newcomers. During his career, however, Palmer finished top of the money list on four different occasions. He was also the first man to win $1 million on the US Tour.

On 10 September 1979 he became eligible for the US Seniors Tour. He wasted no time in stamping his authority on the Tour, winning the title in his first year. He has since won nine times, backed by his loyal army of supporters. In 1979 he was made an honorary member of the Royal and Ancient Golf Club, and his contribution to golf was further recognized in 1981 when he received the Walter Hagen Award.

LEFT: *Arnold Palmer at the peak of his career in 1964.*

ABOVE RIGHT: *Palmer after winning his first British Open title, at Royal Birkdale in 1961.*

RIGHT: *This long putt at Augusta's 13th in 1964 came agonizingly close. Nevertheless Arnie still went on to win his fourth Masters title.*

OVERLEAF: *Palmer during the 1987 US Masters. The winning may have stopped but his popularity and charisma have not waned in more than 20 years.*

Willie Park Senior & Junior

Willie Park Senior

On 17 October 1860 Willie Park Senior earned his place in golfing history by heading the field of eight players to win the inaugural British Open over three rounds at Prestwick's 12-hole course.

Over the first eight years of the Open he and his great rival, 'Old Tom' Morris, dominated the championship, with seven wins between them. Park beat Morris into second place in 1863 and in 1866 he won his third title by beating David Park by two shots. His fourth title came nine years later when he beat Bob Martin by two strokes. Between 1860 and 1868 he never finished lower than fourth.

ABOVE: *Willie Park Senior.*
RIGHT: *Willie Park Junior (seated third from left).*

Born in Musselburgh, Willie Park was one of the great putters of his day. The Park family was to become famous for winning the Open – Willie's brother Mungo took the title in 1874 and his son, Willie Junior, took the title twice, in 1887 and 1889. Willie Park Senior will be remembered, too, as a great money-match player. He placed a longstanding advertisement in *Bell's Life*, for more than 20 years, challenging any golfer in the world to play him for £100 – not surprisingly, he had few takers.

His last Open appearance was in 1878 at the age of 44. After that he devoted much of his time to developing his son's game. Willie Park, the first British Open champion, was 69 when he died in 1903.

Willie Park Junior

Willie Park Junior was born into a golfing family in Musselburgh, Scotland in 1864. Coached by his father (Willie Senior), four times winner of the Open, Willie Junior was 16 when he turned professional.

He took the professional's job at Ryton and competed in his first Open at Prestwick in 1881, finishing joint fifth. He returned to his hometown of Musselburgh in 1883 and set up business as a club and ball maker, producing a wry-necked putter which was to be used by professionals for many years to come.

Like his father, Park was an outstanding putter. He won the first of his two British Open titles in 1887 when he beat Bob Martin by one stroke at Prestwick. When he won again two years later, it was over his home course at Musselburgh. On that occasion he beat Andrew Kirkaldy of St Andrews by five shots in a 36-hole play-off.

An excellent sportsman, Park was the first professional golfer to write a book on the subject, *The Game of Golf*, and he was also the first professional to become involved in golf course design – Sunningdale is one of the courses he helped design.

He died in Edinburgh in 1925 at the age of 61 following a nervous disorder. Willie's daughter Doris maintained the family's golfing tradition by becoming a well-known international and championship golfer, playing for Scotland from 1922 to 1938.

Jerry Pate

Jerry Pate will be immortalized in golfing history by a photograph in which he is shown diving fully clothed into the lake alongside the 18th green at the Cordova Course, Tennessee. He was diving to celebrate his win in the 1981 Danny Thomas-Memphis Classic, his first Tour event for three years.

Pate was an outstanding prospect when he joined the US Tour in 1976. He had won the Amateur title at his first attempt in 1974 and been a Walker Cup player the following year. As a Rookie his first-year winnings of $153,000 established a new record which was only bettered six years later by Hal Sutton in 1982. But even more significant were Pate's victories in the 1976 US and Canadian Opens, two of the game's biggest tournaments.

The US Open took place at Duluth in his native Georgia. Pate finished in great style, placing a five-iron shot from the rough to within two feet of the pin for a birdie putt and the title. Two weeks later his closing round score of 63 in the Canadian Open earned him a four-stroke win over Jack Nicklaus.

Pate won the Phoenix and Southern Opens in his second year and retained the Southern Open in 1978, but there was a hiatus until the win in the Danny Thomas-Memphis Classic. The win took his earnings past the $1 million mark, making him, at 27 years 9 months, the youngest player in golfing history to achieve that record.

Shortly after winning the 1982 Tournament Players Championship at Sawgrass (when Pate repeated his aquatic feat of the previous year), his career was threatened by a severe neck injury. He underwent many tests but it was not until the spring of 1985 that a torn cartilage in the left shoulder was diagnosed. After surgery he played golf again, but with little success, and in 1986 he underwent further surgery. One can only hope he will recover from his shoulder problems to repeat some of those great moments of the 1970s.

RIGHT: *One of 19 children, Calvin Peete found golf by accident.*

LEFT: *On this occasion Jerry Pate is not indulging in aquatic antics but in conventional sand play instead.*

Calvin Peete

As a child Calvin Peete broke his left elbow in an accident and he has never been able to straighten his left arm since that day. A good straight left arm is one of the essentials for good play, but Peete has defied all logic, as well as a physical handicap, to become one of the most consistent drivers in the world.

Peete was brought up in Detroit in a family of 19 children. He dropped out of school at an early age in order to get a job and bring in much needed money to the household. While he was working as a traveling salesman one of his clients introduced Peete to golf. That was in 1966 when he was 23 years of age. He fell in love with the game instantly and sought to emulate his great hero Jack Nicklaus.

Peete set his heart on becoming a professional and joining the US Tour. It was five years before he achieved that first goal and another four before he got through the Tour qualifying school. That was in 1975, but he then had to wait nearly four years for his first win, the 1979 Greater Milwaukee Open. Since then he has won 12 Tour events, including the coveted Tournament Players Championship in 1985 and the Tournament of Champions in 1986.

Peete has finished high on the money list since 1979, including three top-five finishes. In 1987 he slipped out of the top 50 for the first time in nine years and failed to register a win for the first time since 1981. Nevertheless, he still managed to show his high level of consistent driving by topping the US Tour Driving Statistics for the seventh consecutive year.

Henry Picard

Henry Picard had a perfect swing which was to make him one of the most consistent winners in the United States between 1934 and 1945. During that time he won 27 Tour events, a figure that today, more than 40 years later, keeps him well within the top-twenty Tour winners of all time.

He won his first event, the North and South Open, in 1934, and played in the inaugural Masters the same year. He should have won the title a year later when he led by four at the halfway stage, after opening with rounds of 67-68, but he fell away badly. In 1935 he made his Ryder Cup debut, joining the team again two years later.

Picard *did* win the Masters in 1938 when he beat Ralph Guldahl and Harry Cooper by two, in what was Ben Hogan's first Masters. The following year he beat Byron Nelson in the PGA Championship at Pomonok, New York, with birdies at the 36th and at the first extra hole. He was top money winner that year as well as the winner of six events.

Ill health curtailed his tournament play in 1940, and his last attempt at a major was at the age of 43 when he took part in the 1950 US Masters. But by that stage Picard was past his best. In 1961 he was honored with induction into golf's Hall of Fame.

BELOW: *The dapper-looking Henry Picard on his way to beating Byron Nelson at the first extra hole to win the 1939 US PGA title.*

Gary Player

Gary Player's devastating play has been delighting huge galleries of fans for more than 30 years. Not only has he been a fine ambassador for his native South Africa but a credit to the game.

Player has won every honor the game of golf can offer. He has won 21 times on the US Tour, an outstanding record for a non-American, a figure which might have been much greater if he had been less intent on playing golf in other countries and in spending time with his family, wife Vivienne and six children.

Gary Player established himself as the best non-American golfer in the world. At an early age he developed a beautiful swing that has remained unaltered throughout his career. He has also earned a reputation for being a great sand player. To achieve this he used to spend many hours practicing nothing but playing out of bunkers, insisting on continuing until he had holed a shot from the trap.

Since 1956 Gary Player has won his native South African Open no fewer than 13 times; in Britain he has become a match-play specialist, winning the World Match-Play Championship at Wentworth a record five times between 1965 and 1973. But it is in the majors that Player has shown his true ability to beat the best golfers in the world.

Along with Arnold Palmer and Jack Nicklaus, he formed golf's third 'Great Triumvirate,' after Braid-Taylor-Vardon and Hogan-Snead-Nelson. In 1959 he won the British Open with a final round 68, beating the top Belgian Flory van Donck and Britain's Fred Bullock

ABOVE: *Gary Player after the first of his three British Open wins, at Muirfield in 1959.*
BELOW: *Player competes with Palmer in the semifinal of the 1964 Match-Play at Wentworth.*
RIGHT: *Gary Player looking a little concerned about where the ball has gone.*

achieved a remarkable recovery shot – playing a nine iron to within four feet of the pin after a bad first shot, he birdied to earn himself the title.

Player won his second Masters in 1974, ten years after his first, when he won by two from a very tight finish. A couple of months later he won his third British Open – all three had been won in different decades – when he opened with rounds of 69-68 at Lytham to defeat Britain's Peter Oosterhuis.

His ninth and most recent major was the 1978 Masters. He was 42 years of age at the time and became the oldest winner of the title, until Jack Nicklaus claimed the record in 1986. In winning this, his third Masters, Player had to haul back a seven-shot deficit during the final round – he delivered seven birdies at the tough last ten holes, to win by one from three men, including Hubert Green and Tom Watson.

At the 1984 PGA Championship at Shoal Creek Gary Player showed that he is still a force to be reckoned with, even though he is a Senior. He shot a championship record 63 in the second round, to tie in second place behind Lee Trevino. His fine playing in 1987 brought him the US Seniors title. With such a consistent record behind him many would agree that Gary Player stands a very good chance of becoming the first man over the age of 50 to win a major.

ABOVE: *What! no cap? The new-look Gary Player during the 1987 Masters.*
RIGHT: *Gary with his caddy, son Wayne, who is now following in his father's footsteps as a fine golfer.*

by two shots. Player had first captured the hearts of US fans in 1957, and in 1961 he became the first foreign player to win the Masters by beating Arnold Palmer and Charlie Coe by one shot. He won his third *different* major a year later when he won the PGA Championship by one from Bob Goalby.

In 1965 Player became the third man since Gene Sarazen and Ben Hogan to win all four majors when he lifted the US Open at Bellerive, beating Australian Kel Nagle in an 18-hole play-off. He held the further distinction of becoming the first non-American to win the prestigious Open since Ted Ray in 1920.

Over the next 13 years Gary was to add to his total of major championships. First he beat Nicklaus and Bob Charles in a high-scoring British Open over the long Carnoustie course in 1968. Next he won the US PGA title in 1972, beating Tommy Aaron and Jim Jamieson by two. At Oakland Hills' 16th hole in the final round he

Ted Ray

Had it not been for the formidable competition provided by the 'Great Triumvirate' of Braid, Taylor and Vardon, Ted Ray's record would surely have been more impressive than a solitary British Open win. He did, however, achieve something only Vardon (and later, Tony Jacklin) achieved, and that was to become a British winner of the US Open.

Like Vardon, Ray was born on the British island of Jersey. Inspired by the great man's success, Ray himself gave notice that he would succeed Vardon as golf's second great Channel Islander when he was runner-up to James Braid in the prestigious News of the World Tournament in 1901.

Ray followed Vardon as the professional at Ganton, Yorkshire, but in 1912 he moved to Oxhey. That year he went on to win the Open after trying for 13 years, beating Vardon by four shots at Muirfield.

Runner-up to John Taylor at Hoylake the following year, he also gave the United States a taste of his skills in the US Open at Brookline. After a play-off involving Vardon and the unknown American amateur Francis

Ouimet, the two Britons had to be content with second and third places. In 1920, however, Ray took the coveted American crown at the Inverness Club, Ohio when he beat a notable group of men – Vardon, Jack Burke, Leo Diegel and Jock Hutchison – by one shot. At 43 years 4 months he was the oldest winner of the title, a record that stood more than 60 years until surpassed by Ray Floyd in 1986.

Ray competed in his last British Open in 1925 at the age of 48 and tied for second place behind American winner Jim Barnes. Two years later he was honored when he was appointed captain of the first British Ryder Cup team.

A giant of a man, both on and off the golf course, Ray constantly held a pipe between his teeth, supposedly to calm the nerves which had cost him so many tournaments before he began smoking. His style was unorthodox, with a drive which was often wild, but his recovery shots, particularly with the niblick (similar to a present-day wedge), were devastating. He retired in 1940 and died three years later at the age of 66.

RIGHT: *Ted Ray, the last British winner of the US Open before Tony Jacklin, at Gleneagles in 1922.*

Dai Rees

Allan Robertson

If any British schoolboy in the 1950s had been asked to name five well-known sportsmen he would in all probability have said Stanley Matthews, Denis Compton, Gordon Richards, Roger Bannister and Dai Rees. Such was the standing of Rees as Britain's leading golfer at the time, that he was considered alongside such outstanding sportsmen.

Standing just 5 feet 7 inches, Dai Rees made up for any lack of physique with his great determination and aggression. In a career that spanned 50 years he won most major British tournaments, including the PGA Match-Play title four times between 1936 and 1950. But the one title he most wanted, the Open, he never managed to win. He did, however, come close many times, finishing second three times – in 1953 to Ben Hogan, in 1954 to Peter Thomson and in 1961, when aged 48, to Arnold Palmer, by just one shot.

Dai Rees captained the British Ryder Cup team a record five times. His debut as a member of the team was in 1937 when he had a memorable win over Byron Nelson. Even more memorable was 1957, when Rees captained the team that won the Ryder Cup at Lindrick – the last British victory until 1985.

Rees was not the best of stylists, nor was he a great putter, but his play with a wood off the fairway was second to none, and it was this skill that helped him save many shots. In 1973 he was runner-up to Maurice Bembridge at the Martini Tournament at Barnton. Then two years later, in 1975, he became the South of England Professional Champion at the age of 62.

Rees was honored with the CBE shortly after the 1957 Ryder Cup triumph and in 1976 he was awarded honorary membership of the Royal and Ancient Golf Club. He died in November 1983 at the age of 70, the best postwar British golfer never to have won the British Open.

Allan Robertson will go down in golf history as the first of the great professional players.

Born at St Andrews in 1815, he died in 1859, the year before the first British Open. It was said that the Open was inaugurated as a championship to see who should be Robertson's successor, with Willie Park, the first winner of the Open, and the Morrises, 'Young' and 'Old' Tom, as rival claimants.

Robertson realized the importance of being able to play accurate iron shots to the green. He controlled the family golf club and ball manufacturing business that overlooked the 18th green at St Andrews, and employed as his assistant 'Old Tom' Morris. On the golf course the two golfers were invincible and it is said that Robertson never lost a four-man challenge match.

One of the most famous matches Robertson and Morris engaged in was against the Musselburgh brothers, Jamie and Willie Dunn. Played over three courses at 36 holes per course, the St Andrews pair won the deciding match at North Berwick, even though they had been four down with eight to play.

Morris fell out with Robertson and left the business and eventually moved to Prestwick, but they continued their association on the golf course as the outstanding duo of the era.

ABOVE LEFT: *Dai Rees driving from the first tee at Oxhey in Hertfordshire in 1936.*
BELOW: *One of the first golfing greats, Allan Robertson. Sadly he died the year before the first British Open.*

Doug Sanders

Doug Sanders must surely rank as the finest golfer never to have won a major. Of the 21 players who have won 20 or more US Tour events, he is the only one not to have collected one of the 'big four' titles, although he came close on four occasions.

The first time was in the 1959 US PGA at Minneapolis when he finished joint second, one shot behind the unknown Bob Rosburg. Two years later he lost the US Open by one shot when he tied for second place behind the winner Gene Littler. Next he lost the British Open at Muirfield by one shot in 1966 when, again, he came joint second with Britain's Dave Thomas, behind the winner Jack Nicklaus.

It was Nicklaus who deprived Sanders of victory again in the 1970 Open at St Andrews. Having played a magnificent shot out of the bunker to stop dead near the hole at the infamous Road Hole, Sanders came to the 18th green needing to get down in two to win the title, and so become the first pre-qualifier to win the tournament. He left his first putt just two feet short of the hole. But when he putted for the championship he missed and a further 18 holes became necessary. In the play-off Nicklaus drove through the 18th, but chipped back and holed for a birdie and victory by one stroke from the dejected Sanders. Sanders' missed putt at St Andrews that day was to become one of the most famous misses in recent golf history.

Born in Cedartown, Georgia, in 1933, Sanders showed early promise when he won the 1956 Canadian Open as an amateur. He turned professional the following year and joined the US Tour, continuing his success by becoming in the first half of the 1960s one of the Tour's top money winners.

On reaching his 50th birthday in 1983 he joined the Seniors Tour and lost no time in winning the $25,000 World Seniors Invitational in his 'Rookie Year.' Sanders had one of the shortest swings in golf, but he was still talented enough to win 20 tournaments, even if he failed to win a major.

BELOW: *Doug Sanders during the 1972 British Open at Muirfield. He finished fourth.*

Gene Sarazen

When Gene Sarazen appeared in his first British Open at Troon in 1923 he suffered the embarrassment of not qualifying. When he made a nostalgic return 50 years later he played one of those golf shots that will remain immortalized forever.

At Troon's famous 'Postage Stamp' eighth hole in 1973, he played a lofted club from the tee. Seconds later the roar of the crowd told him the ball had entered the hole – a truly memorable and exciting moment in the 71-year-old golfer's career. Interestingly, at the same hole the next day Sarazen found a bunker but chipped in for a two.

Famous for his plus-fours as well as for his bunker shots, Gene Sarazen was one of the giants of golf. Along with Walter Hagen and Bobby Jones, he dominated the game in the 1920s. 'The Squire,' as Sarazen was nicknamed, was the first man to win all four majors and when he won his first, the US Open at Skokie in 1922, he was only 20 years 4 months old, the second youngest winner of the title.

He added the PGA title that year and in 1923 retained it with an impressive win over Hagen at the 38th hole at Pelham, New York. After his first trip to Britain for that year's Open he determined to win the title. He came close in 1928 when he finished runner-up to Hagen at St George's. His ambition was,

ABOVE: *Gene Sarazen with his wife on board the* Mauretania *en route to England in 1924.*

however, fulfilled four years later when he led from start to finish to win the one and only Open to be played at Prince's.

Sarazen won a third US PGA title in 1933 when he beat Willie Goggin 5 and 4 (he came close to winning it in 1930 when he lost the final to Tommy Armour), and in 1934 was runner-up to Olin Dutra in the US Open at Merion. He completed his grand slam of majors in 1935 when he beat the 1934 runner-up Craig Wood in a play-off in the second playing of the Masters at Augusta. During the final round Sarazen played another of golf's great shots when he holed a four-wood from 200 yards for a double-eagle two at the par-5 15th. It is still one of the most talked about shots in golf.

With seven majors to his name, Sarazen nearly achieved an eighth in 1940 in the US Open at Cleveland, Ohio, but he lost the play-off to Lawson Little.

Sarazen continued playing long after his contemporaries had retired. Had he not contracted pleurisy in his youth Sarazen might never have become one of the world's greatest golfers – for it was only while recuperating that he turned to the game, and in so doing, found his career.

Densmore Shute

Densmore Shute was one of the many golfers who turned professional in the late 1920s after seeing the success of Walter Hagen, Gene Sarazen and Bobby Jones. But because of the glut of new talent around, he had to wait five years before winning his first major.

In 1928 he joined the professional ranks and came close to winning the PGA title in 1931, losing the final to Gene Sarazen's former caddie, Tom Creavy. Two years later Shute celebrated the first of several great golfing moments when he won the British Open at St Andrews, but his career had not been without its agonizing moments.

The agony came at Southport in the 1933 Ryder Cup. On the final green he had a putt against Syd Easterbrook to win the trophy for the United States. He missed but had the return putt for a half, and to tie the match. Astonishingly, he missed and the cup went to Great Britain. Two weeks later, the agony turned to delight when he beat Craig Wood in the first all-American play-off, to win the Open at St Andrews. Shute's four rounds were all 73 – the first and only time the Open champion has returned four identical rounds.

There was a three-year wait before his next major, the PGA title, which he retained in 1937 by beating 'Jug' McSpaden at the 37th. No other golfer has since successfully retained the PGA title. Although Shute failed to win the US Open he came close on two occasions – in 1939 when he finished third in the three-man play-off involving Craig Wood and the winner Byron Nelson; and in 1941 when he was runner-up to Wood.

Born in Cleveland, Ohio, in 1904 Densmore Herman Shute died in 1974, at the age of 69.

RIGHT: *Inspired by the success and popularity of such men as Walter Hagen and Bobby Jones, Densmore Shute joined the professional ranks in 1928.*

Scott Simpson

ABOVE: *The cool and unflappable Scott Simpson who made a name for himself with his successes in 1987.*

Jack Nicklaus once remarked that while Scott Simpson might lose to other players, he would never lose to himself; he would always remain calm and controlled, unruffled by the tensions of the game.

A quiet and religious man, Simpson carved his name alongside the golfing greats by winning the 1987 US Open at the Olympic Club, San Francisco. There were many who were surprised at his victory, but not those on the US Tour who felt a major win was long overdue for the talented player. As he went into the final round, Simpson had posted 71, 68, 70 and was two behind Tom Watson who had achieved a fine second round 65. In the final 18 holes Simpson putted with a vengeance, picking up a shot at the 16th, holing out in two from the bunker at 17, and parring the 18th. Watson needed a birdie to tie on 18 but narrowly missed; the victory went to Simpson.

Scott Simpson's golfing career began when he won the NCAA title twice and was a member of the US Walker Cup team. In 1977 he turned professional and he won his first Tour event, the Western Open, in 1980. Since winning the Greater Greensboro Open in 1987 his season winnings have continued to shoot up rapidly toward the $2 million mark.

Horton Smith

Missouri-born Horton Smith burst on to the golf scene in 1928. When he won the Oklahoma City Open at the age of 20 years 5 months old, he was the third youngest winner ever on the US Tour. That winter he won eight tournaments and emerged top of the money list.

His success gained him Ryder Cup selection in 1929. At 21 years 4 days he became the youngest Ryder Cup player to play for the US team, a record which stands today. In 1933 and 1935 he was selected again.

Between 1928 and 1941 he managed to win 30 Tour events, and is today 11th in the all-time list of winners on the US circuit. Even with 30 Tour wins to his credit, Horton Smith will be remembered primarily as the man who was the first winner of the Masters.

In 1934, thanks to a birdie and a par at the last two holes, he beat Craig Wood by one to win the coveted title. Two years later he became the first double winner of the Masters when he made up seven shots on Harry Cooper over the last two rounds, before going on to beat his rival by one at Augusta.

A prominent member of the US PGA Committee for over 20 years, he became President in 1952. Five years later serious illness struck Smith and he never fully recovered. He died in 1963 at the age of 55.

BELOW: *Horton Smith, the first Masters champion.*

Sam Snead

When Sam Snead won the 1965 Greater Greensboro Open it was his 84th win on the US Tour. At the same time he became the oldest winner of the Tour (he was 52 years and 10 months at the time) and the win came 29 years after his first Tour success, the 1936 Virginia Closed Professional Championship. No other golfer has enjoyed as long or as successful a career on the Tour as Snead.

Born in Hot Springs, Virginia, in 1912, 'Slammin' Sam' played his part, along with Byron Nelson and Ben Hogan, in dominating US golf in the immediate postwar years. But, while his two rivals drifted away from competitive play in the 1950s, Snead continued competing at the highest level and was to become the link between that trio and golf's next great threesome, Palmer, Nicklaus and Player. In 1960 and 1962 the chain was linked when Snead and Palmer won the World Cup for the United States.

Winning was certainly Sam Snead's trademark and his list of accompanying honors is truly impressive: he was Player of the Year in 1949, the Vardon Trophy winner four times, a member of eight Ryder Cup teams, and he was inducted into the Hall of Fame in 1953. He topped the money list three times during his career, in 1938, 1949 and 1950, and between 1937 and 1953 never finished lower than 18th. In 1974, after finishing joint third in the PGA Championship, he was 49th on the money list. As recently as 1979 he was still winning money on the regular Tour.

Yet for all his success – he has achieved a record 84 wins on the US Tour and an estimated 135 worldwide –

ABOVE: *Wherever Sam Snead went, so did the fans.*
BELOW: *His putting style may have been unorthodox but it was certainly effective.*

the one title he has never won is the US Open. Undoubtedly the finest golfer never to have won the title, he has been runner-up on four occasions, including his debut in 1937. But Snead did win seven majors during his illustrious career.

The first was the 1942 PGA Championship at Seaview, New Jersey, when he beat Jim Turnesa 2 and 1. He followed that by winning the first postwar British Open in 1946. Two more PGA titles, and two Masters wins, came Snead's way before his finest win in 1954, when he took his third Masters and became, at 41 years 11 months, the oldest winner of the title.

That was the 69th win of Snead's career. He was in his forties and was having to compete with a new generation of talented players. Nevertheless over the next 20 years he increased his number of wins by 15 to 84. Then he went yet again into the record books in the 1979 Quad Cities Tournament when he became the first man on Tour to shoot his own age. He shot a round of 66; he was 67 at the time!

As a Senior he added 13 more wins to his already impressive total, including the PGA Seniors title on six occasions and the World Seniors five times. When he won the 1982 Legends of Golf with Don January, Sam Snead was 70 years of age – and still managed to get his name into the record books.

Craig Stadler

In his first six years on the US golf circuit Craig Stadler showed increasingly each year that he had the ability to break away from the pack and move away from being simply a very good player to something much rarer – a superstar. With victories in 1982 in the Tucson Open, US Masters, Kemper Open and World Series of Golf, when he became the 37th man to win $1 million in a career, he succeeded in becoming the top money winner in the United States.

Stadler put his improved year down to two factors. Firstly he had sacrificed distance with his drive for accuracy, and secondly his putting had improved noticeably and was at its best all season. Two of the victories were won after play-offs, over Ray Floyd in the World Series and over Dan Pohl in the Masters. At Augusta he had a six-shot lead with nine to play but bogeyed the 12th, 14th, 16th and 18th holes; Pohl, playing his first Masters, forced a play-off. When Stadler eventually won the sudden-death, the organizers struggled to find a winner's green jacket to fit his size, as he weighed over 200 pounds.

'The Walrus,' as Stadler is nicknamed for his rotund figure and bushy mustache, has won only one US tournament since 1982, the 1984 Byron Nelson Classic, but he continues to be a regular money winner, with more than $2 million in earnings behind him.

When he joined the professional ranks Stadler had an outstanding amateur career behind him. He was the World Junior Champion in 1971 and the US Amateur Champion in 1973; in 1975 he ended his amateur days with Walker Cup selection. In 1976 he joined the Tour, where he had to work not only on improving his game but on controlling his temper. His first Tour win did not come until 1980 when he won the Bob Hope Desert Classic which he followed up immediately with the Greater Greensboro Open. Suddenly Craig Stadler was up there along with the best on the Tour, a position he has held ever since.

LEFT: *There are no prizes for guessing why Craig Stadler is called 'The Walrus.'*

Curtis Strange

Curtis Strange will be remembered as the man who gave the 1985 US Masters to Bernhard Langer. With nine holes to play he went into a four-shot lead – then he bogeyed at the 10th only to follow this up with a further disaster at the 13th when he shot into the lake. Two holes later he found water again, and with it went his chances of winning his first major. Strange had come very close to what would have been one of the most remarkable pieces of scoring the great championship has seen, because he had opened with an 80 and then gone on to score a 65 and a 68.

Many players would have let that disappointment affect their game, but not Curtis Strange. Inspired to put his house in order he finished the season as the biggest money winner in one season the US Tour had ever known. Wins in the Honda Classic, the Las Vegas Invitational and the Canadian Open pushed his earnings to $542,321, $12,000 more than Tom Watson's 1980 record sum.

Ever since his college days he has had a burning desire to win and it is that desire that has taken him to, and kept him at, the top. Strange's father was also a professional golfer but he died when Curtis was 14. The following year Curtis won his first tournament, the Virginia State Junior Championship. The biggest thrill of his amateur career came in 1975 when he won the Eastern Amateur title – in 1957 his father had been the inaugural winner of the event. After playing in the World Amateur Team Championship and the Walker Cup, Curtis Strange turned professional in 1976. He joined the Tour a year later and in 1979 won his first event, the Pensacola Open. At the end of a season-long battle with Paul Azinger for the position of top money-winner on the US Tour, Curtis emerged on top.

In 11 seasons Strange has established himself as one of the biggest earners from the game and he has already passed the $3 million mark. Two wins in the 1980 season elevated him to third position on the money list and he has since won $200,000-plus every season. Altogether Curtis has won 12 US Tour events in nine years, and has been a winner every year since 1983. While 1986 was in no way as successful as his outstanding season the year before, he still won nearly $250,000 and was the Houston Open Champion. A return to form in 1987 saw him lift the Canadian Open, the St Jude Classic and the World Series of Golf to make him the top money winner for a second time, with a record $925,941, and gain him a third successive Ryder Cup selection.

LEFT: *With season's winnings of more than $900,000 in 1987, Curtis Strange not only finished first but established a US Tour record.*

Hal Sutton

When Hal Sutton burst onto the golf scene many people commented on how like Jack Nicklaus he was, in looks and style. Sutton admits he modeled himself on Nicklaus; he certainly shares the same determination to succeed.

Having a wealthy father helped Hal Sutton concentrate and develop his golf game from the age of 11. His father Howard, an oil magnate, encouraged his son in all his sporting activities at school. Although Hal was a good, class footballer, he soon decided his temperament would be better suited to golf in which he would not be part of a team and winning or losing would be his own destiny.

Sutton's career got off to a fine start when he became US Amateur Champion in 1980. The following year, after a spell spent working with his father, he decided to turn professional. By 1982 he was on the US Tour and had amassed impressive winnings of more than $237,000, a record for a Rookie.

ABOVE: *Hal Sutton with the US PGA Championship trophy after he had beaten Jack Nicklaus by one shot to win at the Riviera Club, Los Angeles, in 1983.*

Sutton's first Tour win was in the Walt Disney World Golf Classic during his first full season. In 1983 he increased his earnings to $426,000 to become the top money-winner in the United States. Victories that year in the Tournament Players' Championship and a one-stroke win over Jack Nicklaus in the PGA at Riviera netted him $226,000 alone.

The following year he failed to register a win, slipping to 26th position. By 1985 he had returned to the top eight and was selected for the Ryder Cup team. Since then his standard of play has remained consistently high, and in 1987 he was once again chosen for the Ryder Cup team. His 1987 winnings amounted to a personal best of $477,996 which took his career total past $2 million.

John Henry Taylor

John Henry Taylor was a member of golf's first 'Great Triumvirate' which dominated the game between 1894 and 1914. Known as 'J H,' Taylor played an important part in raising the standards of professional golf and was largely responsible for the formation of the Professional Golfers' Association (PGA) in 1901.

Born in 1871, the son of a Devon laborer, he left school at the young age of 11. After a succession of jobs, as a bootboy, garden boy and mason's laborer, he joined the greenkeeping staff at Westward Ho! when he was 17. He had tried to join the army and navy but was rejected because of poor eyesight, and the Metropolitan Police had rejected him because he was too short. He was, therefore, left with little alternative but to turn to golf.

At the age of 19 he turned professional and moved to Burnham where he became the greenkeeper. It is said that he left home with a borrowed sovereign in search of his fortune – which he was later to find.

Affectionate, and delightful company, Taylor won five British Opens. The first was at Sandwich in 1894 when he became the first non-Scottish professional to win the title. He retained the title at St Andrews a year later. In 1900 he won at St Andrews again, almost completing a British/US double, but his great rival Vardon beat him in the American Open at Chicago. A fourth British title followed in 1909 when Taylor won by four shots from James Braid over the Deal links.

When he won his last Open, at Hoylake in 1913, he was 42 years of age. In addition to his five British Opens, he won the coveted British Professional Match-Play title twice, in 1904 and 1908, the French Open in 1908 and 1909 and the German Open in 1912.

J H spent most of his career as the professional at Royal Mid-Surrey. His son Leslie was his assistant for a period, while a second son, J H, also carried on the family golfing tradition by becoming an Oxford golfing blue. J H Senior retired to Northam where he died at the age of 92 in February 1963, the last surviving member of the 'Great Triumvirate.'

ABOVE: *One of the three men known as the 'Great Triumvirate,' John Henry Taylor. Born in Devon, he was generally referred to by his initials 'JH.'*

LEFT: *Part of the service Harrods offered to customers purchasing golf clubs in 1914 was instructional help from leading professionals of the day. Here J H Taylor is seen offering advice to a potential customer.*

Peter Thomson

LEFT: *Five-times winner of the British Open, Australian Peter Thomson was just one win short of Harry Vardon's all-time record. Only Tom Watson has since equaled Thomson's postwar record in the championship.*

Peter Thomson's record in the British Open is undoubtedly the most outstanding since the days of the 'Great Triumvirate' of Vardon, Taylor and Braid. Between 1954 and 1965 he won the title five times and his achievement of three consecutive wins, from 1954 to 1956, has only been matched by one other man, 'Young Tom' Morris, 80 years earlier.

For his first four wins Thomson, admittedly, did not have to contend with the strong opposition from the United States which the Open winner of today faces, but he still had to beat formidable opponents like his great South African rival Bobby Locke, Britons Dai Rees, Harry Weetman and Eric Brown and the top Belgian Flory van Donck. But by the time he won for the fifth time in 1965, a strong field of American challengers had gathered and Thomson answered the critics who had questioned his ability to compete with top quality opposition.

Born in Melbourne in 1929, Thomson could certainly claim to be the best golfer produced by Australia prior to the arrival of David Graham and Greg Norman. His superb judgment and long-iron play were to account for much of his success. When he competed in his first professional tournament, the 1950 New Zealand Open, he won. He went on to win the title nine times in all, as

well as winning the Australian Open three times. The last time was in 1972 when he was 43.

But it was in the British Open that Thomson became a legend. He first competed in 1951, finishing sixth. Between 1952 and 1958 his performance was remarkable – he never finished lower than second. No other golfer can claim such a record of consistency in the world's top tournament.

In comparison, Thomson's record on the US circuit has been disappointing. His long-iron game was not suited to American courses and he won only one tournament in the United States, the 1956 Texas Open. Since joining the Seniors Tour, however, Thomson has thrilled American galleries, and has won more money on the Tour than he won in his entire career as a regular tournament professional – a record that includes five British Open wins and more than 50 tournaments worldwide.

In 1979 Thomson retired from tournament play, turning his attention to golf journalism, golf course architecture and television commentating. He has also been involved in politics and in work to curb drug addiction, and has served the Australian PGA. He was awarded the CBE and in 1982 was made an honorary member of the Royal and Ancient.

Lee Trevino

With his own brand of skill, wit, and humor Lee Trevino has, over the past 25 years, made an immense contribution to the game of golf. Today he remains one of the most outstanding characters, not only in the world of golf but in the world of sport as a whole.

Trevino was born in Dallas, of Mexican stock, in December 1939. He used to caddy at a nearby course when only eight years old and, even at that early age, he was digesting the science of the game that he was later to perfect in his own way. Trevino was completely self-taught and from the age of 14 had no ambition in life other than to earn his living playing golf.

In 1960, he turned professional, but his first Tour win took eight years to arrive. And when it came, it came with style, when Trevino took the US Open at Oak Hill. His achievement is even more remarkable when one remembers it was Jack Nicklaus that he beat, and by four strokes.

Trevino's list of achievements since then has been enormous. He has won 27 Tour events and has represented the United States in six Ryder Cup matches, including once as the nonplaying captain in 1985 – the first time in 28 years that the United States *lost*! Trevino thrives on the 'big-match' environment as his

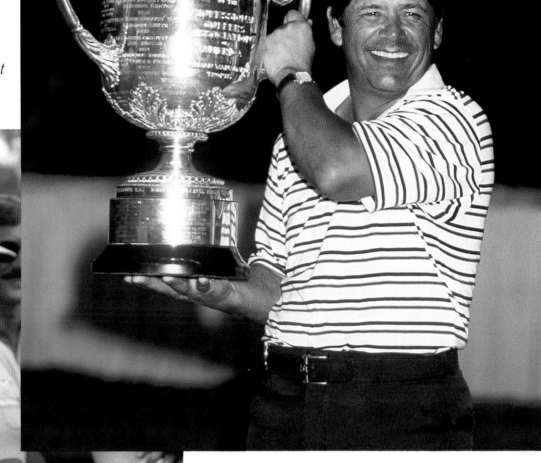

RIGHT: *One of the many great moments in the career of Lee Trevino, as he wins the 1984 US PGA title aged 44.*

BELOW: *A joker and a crowd puller, Lee Trevino is one of golf's great characters.*

BELOW LEFT: *Trevino in a more serious mood. But serious or joking, he is still a winner.*

record of six major championships shows. He has won the British Open, the US Open and the PGA Championship, each twice, but the Masters has eluded him.

Trevino enjoyed his greatest moments in the early 1970s. In 1970 he topped the US money list for the one and only time in his career. The following year he won, within the space of three weeks, the US, Canadian and British Opens to complete the finest hat-trick of wins professional golf has seen. The British Open win was especially memorable as Trevino faced a classic encounter with Taiwan's 'Mr Lu.'

Trevino retained his British Open in 1972, when he holed two chips and a bunker shot to destroy Britain's Tony Jacklin, and in 1974 he won the PGA Championship. It was 10 years before he won another major, but he had a history of back trouble, stemming from the time he was struck by lightning during the 1975 Western Open. When he won the PGA for the second time, in 1984, it was his first Tour win for 3½ years. He was 44 years old at the time, and it is not surprising that he regards this as the finest win of his career.

Bob Tway

Bob Tway burst onto the golfing scene in 1986 and was quickly labeled golf's next superstar. By the following year, however, his performance had dropped and he had joined the pack of also-rans. He remains nevertheless a very good golfer, with an ice-cool nerve, a perfect swing and a fine putting style.

Born in Oklahoma City, Tway picked up his first golf club when he was seven, inspired by his father and grandfather. He was outstanding as a college player and turned professional in 1981 at the age of 22. It was four years before he joined the US Tour, during which time he played in Europe and Asia.

His first season on the US Tour saw him earn a comfortable $164,000, but without registering a win. The tables were turned in 1986 when he won his first tournament, the Shearson Leman Bros-Andy Williams Open. He went on to follow that up with three more wins and earnings of $652,000 which put him second to Greg Norman by a mere $516. To crown his achievements he was named PGA Golfer of the Year for 1986.

The fourth of his 1986 wins was in the PGA Championship at Inverness, Ohio, and he won with a shot that will be talked about for many years. The championship was a two-man contest between the top money-winners on the Tour, Norman and Tway. As they teed off at the 72nd they were level. Tway found the rough with his second shot but chipped into the hole for a birdie three and so took the championship.

His perfect swing and good putting style promise an exciting future for this fine golfer.

RIGHT: *Bob Tway, winner of the 1986 US PGA Championship at Inverness, Ohio, awaits his turn to play.*

Harry Vardon

Harry Vardon was a member of the first 'Great Triumvirate' whose influence on golf at the turn of the century extended to both sides of the Atlantic. When Vardon decided to tour the United States in 1900, not only did he win the US Open at Chicago, but he stirred up a great deal of interest in the sport, which was still in its infancy in the States at the time.

Born in Grouville, Jersey, in 1870, Vardon was a caddie at his home course for several years, although at the time he played very little golf. When his younger brother Tom moved to England to become assistant professional at St Anne's, he suggested Harry should make the same move. Consequently in 1890 Harry became assistant at Ripon's nine-hole course. He moved to Bury St Edmunds the following year and in 1893 he appeared in his first British Open, but with little impact. The following year he finished joint fifth. In 1895 he did not compete but in 1896, when professional at Yorkshire's famous Ganton Club, he won the first of his record six titles by beating Taylor by four strokes after a 36-hole play-off at Muirfield.

Between then and 1922 Vardon played in 22 consecutive Opens, achieving 18 top-ten finishes. Vardon's second title was at Prestwick in 1898 and he retained

his title twelve months later, at Sandwich. His fourth win followed at Prestwick in 1903. The year before, Vardon had joined the South Herts Club, where he was to remain the professional up to his death. After his fourth Open win Vardon's game declined but he came back to win the championship, at Prestwick once again, in 1911, and at the same venue three years later he notched up his record sixth win.

In 1913 Vardon entered the US Open at Brookline. He tied for second place with Ted Ray behind the surprise winner, Francis Ouimet. Seven years later Vardon was one of four who tied for second place behind Ray in the same event. Vardon was 50 at the time.

Although he was only a moderate 5 feet 9 inches tall Vardon developed great power with his drive, and this was matched with astonishing accuracy. It was Vardon who popularized the overlapping grip which now bears his name, and he also did much to promote the game at all levels. Harry Vardon, six times winner of the British Open, died in 1937 at the age of 66.

Ken Venturi

Ken Venturi had just one really outstanding moment during his 10-year career on the US Tour, but it was to go down in the annals of golfing history.

It occurred during the 1964 US Open at the Congressional Country Club. Lying two strokes behind Tommy Jacobs after a third round 66, Venturi was near collapse through exhaustion before the start of the final round. This was to be the last occasion the final two rounds were played in one day and Venturi had to be accompanied by a doctor over the final 18 holes. With his legs barely capable of carrying him forward, Venturi resolutely parred the last four holes to beat Jacobs by four shots and win a remarkable Open.

Born in San Francisco in 1931, Venturi was the runner-up in the inaugural USA Junior Championship in 1948, and in 1956 he hit the headlines when he produced the best-ever result by an amateur in the Masters. After leading for three rounds, he started the final round with an eight-shot lead over Jack Burke, but in a dramatic reversal of fortunes Venturi finished with an 80 to Burke's 71, to lose by just one shot.

Venturi turned professional the following year and in 1960 was runner-up in the Masters once again. In the final round he was leading Arnold Palmer by one with two to play, but Palmer birdied the last two, to win by one shot. Venturi succeeded in finishing second on the money list that year to Palmer, but his game started to decline when he changed his swing in an effort to achieve greater distance with his irons. The new approach didn't work and he then found it difficult to revert to his former swing.

By 1964, however, he was once again in top form – he qualified for and won the Open and was named PGA Player of the Year. In 1965 he was selected for the Ryder Cup team, but Venturi's play began to decline once again, this time his ailing hands affecting his performance.

The last of his 14 Tour wins took place in 1966. After that Venturi decided to turn his attentions to commentating on the game for CBS Television.

BELOW: *Two of golf's legends playing together during the 1983 Masters at Augusta, Ken Venturi (teeing off) watched by the 1935 winner, Gene Sarazen.*

Lanny Wadkins

Lanny Wadkins is one of the boldest players currently in world golf. He plays the big shots and it is that approach to the game that has helped him win some of the biggest tournaments and play on some of the sport's most demanding courses.

Lanny's younger brother Bobby is also a professional and fellow member of the US Tour, but it is Lanny, born in Richmond, Virginia, in 1949 who has the better record. He joined the Tour in 1971 and for ten years his fortunes fluctuated. He won his first event in 1972, when he took the Sahara Invitational, and finished 10th on the money list. Two wins in 1973 saw him rise to fifth but in the next three years he was without a win and dropped out of the top 50.

By 1977, however, he was once again winning, in the PGA Championship and in the World Series of Golf, and he jumped to third position on the money list with earnings totaling $244,000. Over the next four years he finished 61st, 10th, 58th and 81st, but since 1982 Lanny Wadkins has achieved nine Tour wins to become one of the biggest winners in the game.

ABOVE: *With his bold approach to the game, Lanny Wadkins has played successfully on some of golf's most demanding courses.*

His most recent major was the 1977 PGA at Pebble Beach, when he won the first ever PGA event over the famous course, beating the seasoned campaigner Gene Littler at the third extra hole. It was the first time sudden death had been used to decide a major championship.

Lanny came close to a second major in 1987 when, yet again, he was involved in a play-off for the PGA Championship at the PGA National. This time he was beaten by Larry Nelson who emerged as the winner at the first extra hole.

During his brilliant career on the golfing circuit the honor that has given him greatest personal satisfaction was being named the PGA Player of the Year in 1985 – he knew the name of Lanny Wadkins had been installed alongside such other great names of golf as Hogan, Snead, Palmer, Nicklaus and Watson.

Tom Watson

LEFT: *Tom Watson's swing has helped keep him at the top of world golf for more than 10 years.*

RIGHT: *Watson after winning his second British Open title in 1977. He beat Jack Nicklaus by one stroke in an epic record-breaking championship at Turnberry.*

Since 1974 Tom Watson has been one of the leading players in the game. When he first emerged as a winner, in the 1974 Western Open, he was being tipped as Jack Nicklaus's successor and from 1977 to 1984 Watson certainly reigned supreme.

Born in Kansas City, Missouri, in 1949, Tom Watson graduated from Stanford University with a degree in psychology. Perhaps more importantly, he was a four-times winner of the Missouri State Amateur golf title, an indication as to where his real talents lay.

A professional since 1971, he had nine memorable years between 1975 and 1983 when he won a stagger-

ing eight majors including a modern-day record five British Open titles, just one short of Harry Vardon's all-time record. In 1975 he beat the unfortunate Australian Jack Newton in a play-off at Carnoustie to win the 1975 British Open.

In 1977 he went on to win his first Masters in what was to prove one of his most satisfying successes when he beat Nicklaus in a head-to-head contest over the last three rounds. He followed that win with a second exciting British Open, at Turnberry in 1977, when he and Nicklaus broke records galore. His winning streak continued when he achieved a third title at

Tom Weiskopf

Muirfield in 1980 and the following year he won a second Masters title, again with Nicklaus trailing in second place.

Tom Watson's outstanding record continued when he completed a US/British Open double in 1982, winning at Pebble Beach and Troon. Once again Nicklaus was runner-up to Watson in the US Open, with Watson playing one of golf's remarkable shots at the 17th on the final day. With his ball five yards from the pin and lying in thickish rough he chipped in to clinch victory from Nicklaus. The most recent of Tom Watson's majors was the 1983 British Open at Royal Birkdale – his fifth British Open victory.

To appreciate Watson's great stature his outstanding record in the major championships must be viewed in conjunction with his other achievements. He was the top money winner in the States for four years in succession, 1977 to 1980, and he was the first golfer to earn more than $500,000 in one season. Although he 'slipped' over the next three years, finishing 12th in

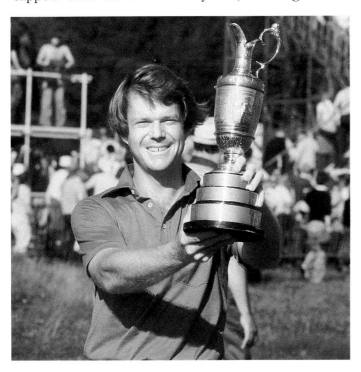

1983, he bounded back in 1984 by winning three Tour events and topping the money list for a fifth time. His record number of 31 Tour wins is the joint ninth best of all time and he is the second biggest money winner in the game, with winnings of more than $4,250,000. He has been the PGA Player of the Year six times and has won the Vardon Trophy three times. Perhaps the greatest compliment paid to Tom Watson was in 1983 and by Jack Nicklaus himself. Nicklaus, captain of the Ryder Cup team, announced that Watson would be playing in every match because his presence alone would be sufficient to intimidate the opposition.

With one of the finest and most fluent swings in modern golf Tom Weiskopf emerged as one of the most consistent players of the 1970s.

Surprisingly for such a talented golfer he won only one of the sport's major championships during a career spanning 20 years, and that was the 1973 British Open at Troon. But that Open win was just a part of his best season which put him third on the US money list.

During an eight-week spell in 1973 he won five

ABOVE: *Tom Weiskopf after winning the 1973 British Open at Troon.*

events: the Colonial National, the Kemper Open, the Philadelphia Classic, the Canadian Open and then, spectacularly, the British Open. Playing at Troon he led from start to finish, displaying a mastery of the damp conditions; his rounds of 68, 67, 71 and 70 were to equal Arnold Palmer's Open record of 276 which had been set at the same course 11 years before.

A member of the US Tour since 1965, Weiskopf won 15 Tour events. His first win was the Andy Williams San Diego Open in 1968. Between 1969 and 1975 he was runner-up in the Masters four times. His best chance of victory was in the 1975 Masters when he led Nicklaus by one going into the final round. On the 72nd green he needed an eight-foot putt to tie with Nicklaus. The putt was dead on line but stopped short, and Tom lost. In 1976 Weiskopf was a runner-up again, in the US Open to Jerry Pate.

Since finishing 22nd on the Tour in 1982 when he won his last event, the Western Open, Tom has cut back on his playing to spend more time with his family and to engage in big-game hunting.

Ian Woosnam

In 1981 Ian Woosnam finished 104th on the European Order of Merit with winnings of £1884. Six years later he had jumped 103 places and won a staggering £330,000 – a new European record. During those six years Woosnam won nine European events including five in 1987.

Born in Shropshire, England, Woosnam was brought up on a farm. Strong arms helped make him one of the longest hitters in world golf – he can hit the ball more than 260 yards from the tee – yet he stands a little over 5 feet 4 inches tall.

Never outstanding as an amateur, he surprised a lot of people when he turned professional in 1976. Their pessimism appeared justified when he failed in his first two attempts to qualify for the European Tour. Eventually in 1978 he joined the Tour; in his first four seasons his winnings amounted only a little over £6000. In 1982, however, the little man with the big swing turned the tables.

He began by winning his first Tour event, the Swiss Open at Crans-sur-Sierre, and then the prestigious Cacharel World Under-25 Championship. With these wins his earnings jumped dramatically to £48,000 and he found himself among the top 10 on the Order of Merit. The following year he held his position and also gained the first of his three Ryder Cup selections. Two years later, Woosnam played a very significant part in helping wrest the Cup from the United States for the first time in 28 years.

Despite being winless in 1985 Woosnam still managed to finish fourth on the Order of Merit, a measure of his consistency. In 1986 he managed just one win, the end-of-season Lawrence Batley Tournament Players Championship; still he held his fourth position in the rankings. In 1987, however, it was nothing but one success after another for Woosnam.

The season was only three weeks old when he won his first tournament, the Jersey Open. A fortnight later he had added the Madrid Open trophy to his collection of triumphs. Victories in the Bell's Scottish Open and the Lancôme Trophy followed before Woosnam flew to the United States to be part of the historic European Ryder Cup team that won at Muirfield Village. In October Woosnam became the first Briton to win the World Match-Play title when he came from behind to beat Sandy Lyle in the final after beating Seve Ballesteros by one hole in a great semifinal. He rounded off the season a month later when he was a member of the Welsh team that won the World Cup for the first time.

LEFT: *In 1987 Ian Woosnam hit the headlines with a run of success that began in April with the Jersey Open and ended in November when he played in the Welsh team that won the World Cup for the first time.*

Fuzzy Zoeller

Fuzzy Zoeller once described himself as, 'Not a great player but a damned good one.' He was being modest in his assessment, for at times he showed flashes of brilliance that only a great player can produce.

Ever smiling and jovial, Fuzzy Zoeller kept a secret for most of his career which was only revealed to the golf public in 1984. A basketball injury during his school days had damaged his back so that for years he played with a constant nagging injury. In 1984 when he was about to start the PGA Championship at Shoal Creek he found he could hardly move. He was taken to hospital and surgery followed; today he plays without the pain he endured for so long.

Zoeller became a professional in 1973 and joined the Tour two years later. He made a notable impact in 1976 when he equaled the 25-year Tour record with eight consecutive birdies in the Quad Cities Open. But it was in 1979 that he first emerged as a truly great player. He won his first Tour event, the San Diego Open, and followed this up by winning the Masters.

He started the final round at Augusta six shots behind Ed Sneed and finished his championship with a 280 to tie for second place with Tom Watson. When Sneed reached the 18th he needed a par for the title. He bogeyed and all three had to play off. Zoeller won at the second extra hole in the first sudden death in the Masters and became the first man to win the title at the first attempt (excluding the first year).

With this win Frank Urban Zoeller firmly established himself on the golfing map, and has since finished regularly in the top 50 of the money list. Even in the year of his bad back, 1984, he finished 40th with winnings of more than $150,000. That year he achieved a second major. In the Open at Winged Foot, the outcome was nearly a reversal of his 1979 Masters triumph. With Australia's Greg Norman breathing down his neck, Zoeller led by three with five to go. At the 18th Norman needed a 40-foot putt to force a play-off. He made the putt but Zoeller played his majestic best to win the 18-hole play-off by eight shots with a 67.

RIGHT: *Fuzzy Zoeller during the 1985 US Open at Oakland Hills. After two rounds he was in contention, but in the end he finished four behind the winner, Andy North.*

Index

Page numbers in *italics* refer to illustrations.

Acknowledgments

The publisher would like to thank Design 23 who designed this book; Melanie Earnshaw, the picture researcher; and Ron Watson, the indexer; as well as the following agencies and individuals for supplying the illustrations (A=above, B=below, C=center, L=left, R=right, T=top):

All-Sport: pages 2-3, 4(TR), 7, 11(both), 14, 15(both), 16(L), 20, 28, 30(R), 31, 35, 38, 47(L), 54, 57, 68, 77, 82, 86(B), 88(T), 94(T), 95(T), 103(TR), 107, 110.
Associated Press: pages 43, 49, 53, 61(L), 67, 69, 72(B), 81(B).
BBC Hulton Picture Library: pages 5(A+R), 12, 17(both), 23, 41, 42, 45, 52, 56, 62, 88(B), 89, 90(T), 96, 100(both), 109(R).
Peter Dazeley: pages 12, 24, 25, 32, 47(R), 63, 65, 70, 74, 78, 84, 102(L), 109(L).
Courtesy Golf Illustrated: pages 36(L), 66.
The Keystone Collection: pages 9, 18(L), 29, 36(R), 40(L), 40-41(C), 44, 46(both), 60(B), 61(R), 72(T), 79, 94(B), 105.
Brian Morgan, Golf Photography International: pages 1, 8(R), 50, 51, 59, 64, 73, 76, 85(L), 87, 95(B), 97, 98, 99, 101, 102-103, 104, 106, 108.
S+G Press Agency; pages 4(BR), 21, 37, 55(L), 75.
St Andrews University Library/Cowie Archive: page 83(both).
The Scotsman Publications: page 86(T).
UPI/Bettmann Newsphotos: pages 4(BR), 5(BL), 10, 30(L), 33, 34, 39, 60(T), 85(R).
US Golf Association: pages 4(C), 8(L), 16(R), 18(R), 19, 22(L), 58.